Fourscore Classics
of
Music Literature

Da Capo Press Music Reprint Series

GENERAL EDITOR

FREDERICK FREEDMAN

VASSAR COLLEGE

Fourscore Classics

of

Music Literature

By GUSTAVE REESE

𝄞 DA CAPO PRESS • NEW YORK • 1970

A Da Capo Press Reprint Edition

This Da Capo Press edition of *Fourscore Classics of Music Literature*
is an unabridged republication of the first edition published in New
York in 1957, and is reprinted by special arrangement with the
Bobbs-Merrill Company, Inc.

ML
160
. R 33

Fourscore Classics
of Music Literature

Fourscore Classics
of Music Literature

By GUSTAVE REESE

A Guide to Selected Original Sources
on Theory and Other Writings on Music
Not Available in English, with Descriptive
Sketches and Bibliographical References

THE LIBERAL ARTS PRESS
NEW YORK

Published at 153 West 72nd Street, New York 23, N. Y.

———————————

Printed in the United States of America

FOREWORD

Gustave Reese, a native of New York, is well known to the students and followers of musicology. His two major contributions to scholarly literature are *Music in the Middle Ages* and *Music in the Renaissance,* but equally valuable have been his occasional essays, his editorial services, and his influence as a teacher. No person could be better suited to present the information contained in this brochure, which runs the gamut of the ages and surveys important monuments of our scholarly heritage.

When the Committee on Music and Musicology of the American Council of Learned Societies, desirous of advancing the cause of musicology in the United States and of attracting increased support for it, devised a series of brochures that might partially achieve these objectives, it was impressed by the inadequate availability, in English translation, of literary source materials, especially of the earlier periods. Many musical treatises (aesthetic, philosophical, technical) remain too long unfamiliar to even the deeply earnest student because of language barriers. How much more difficult is it, then, for the intelligent and interested layman to learn of the major figures who kept the torch of musical learning and speculation burning brightly. In this succinct but comprehensive survey of masterpieces produced by them but not yet available in English, Professor Reese exposes a wide and provocative vista. His own introduction explains his selections and suggests the challenge these untranslated texts offer to all those who wish to see our discipline prosper.

The members of the ACLS Committee on Music and Musicology (until September 30, 1956, called the Committee on Musicology) are Jacques Barzun (Columbia University); Edward Downes (*The New York Times*); Gustave Reese

(New York University); Leo Schrade (Yale University), secretary; Edward N. Waters (Library of Congress), chairman. (At the time this paper was planned and prepared, Manfred Bukofzer was a member of the Committee, Carroll C. Pratt of Princeton University was its chairman, and the undersigned was its secretary.) To this group have come the invaluable aid, counsel, and collaboration of Dr. D. H. Daugherty, Assistant to the Director of the ACLS. The Committee takes pride and satisfaction in Dr. Reese's survey, one of several papers written to broaden our understanding of the art and science of musicology.

EDWARD N. WATERS

CONTENTS

INTRODUCTION

The English-speaking world has found itself especially responsive in recent decades to the attractions of musicology. Partly as a result, partly as a further stimulus, there has come into being an ever-increasing supply of tools upon which the student belonging to that world can draw while breaking open the earlier windings of his path. A body of literature has gradually been taking shape in English such as has long since been available in his own language to the German-speaking student. One type of publication, however, of which there continues to be a notable shortage, is the English translation of basic original source material. The few examples at hand include some of conspicuous excellence, such as the translations contained in Oliver Strunk's *Source Readings in Music History*. But one need only glance rapidly through the bibliographies appended to the thumbnail sketches in the present booklet to recognize how greatly the quantity of complete translations into German exceeds that into English.

To be sure, the conscientious scholar in quest of authority will wish as few barriers as possible between an original writing and himself, and it will be his aim to develop a similar attitude in any student who comes under his influence. But it is unrealistic to feel that the student is necessarily ready to make such an attitude effectual in the earlier stages of his growth, or even that the experienced scholar will not welcome the opportunity of becoming acquainted with a colleague's proposed interpretation of a troublesome passage. Moreover, it is clear that some available translations have reached a reading public far larger than that formed by developing and mature musicologists. An intelligent music lover having no intention of becoming a musicologist is nevertheless a potential reader of important literary sources on music, provided no language barrier stands in his way. A scholar, highly trained in his own specialty, may himself be regarded as much like such a music lover with respect to fields other than his own: the specialist in European Renaissance music, for instance, may well be interested in learning in detail the content of some original document dealing with a body of oriental music in an Asiatic language unfamiliar to him. Potential readers of translated source writings about music include also people whose chief concern with the art is the role it plays in general cultural life and thought. As one examines earlier writings on music, one cannot fail to note the attention paid to subject matter which, to the modern musician or music historian, may appear extraneous or perhaps even fantastic—for example, the music of the spheres, the ethos of the modes, number symbolism, the relation of music to mathematics. But the discussion of such topics, while it seems to have little bearing on the history of music itself as a practiced art, does figure in the history of ideas. Over and above this, it testifies to the older writers' wish to relate music to man as a whole and to the whole of his environment. To these people music was definitely one of the humanities, in fact if not in nomenclature. However wide of the mark they may have been in their quasi-philosophical speculations, they provided, in the broadness of their outlook, an example from which the present-day overprofessionalized musician and music historian might well profit.

On several counts, then, the need exists for a large quantity of English translations, preferably complete, of important source literature on music. It would be a splendid thing if Professor Strunk's fine anthology could be paralleled by series like the *Records of Civilization* published in the field of history by the Columbia University Press, the English translations of classics in different languages and disciplines currently being published in "The Library of Liberal Arts" by the Liberal Arts Press, or the several series of translations into German brought out early in the century by Eugen Diederichs of Jena, such as *Das Zeitalter der Renaissance.*

It is largely for the purpose of stimulating interest in a comparable series in the field of music that the present group of thumbnail sketches has been compiled. Inevitably, of course, the question arises: On which form of the original text should the prospective translator base his work? Among the writings likely to be included in such a series, those of which the original was printed and in only one edition are in the minority. It is all too obvious that there are many more instances in which works come down to us in several variant manuscripts or printed editions. On the other hand, preparation of the hoped-for series would be greatly facilitated by the large number of good modern editions that are available and by the steady output of facsimile reproductions. The task would certainly be lightened, for example, by the series initiated in 1922 for the publication in facsimile of some of the treasures belonging to the Paul Hirsch Music Library, originally at Frankfort-on-Main (attention being divided about equally between writings on music and music itself); by the *Collezione di Trattati e Musiche Antiche edite in fac-simile,* inaugurated a few years later by the Bollettino Bibliografico Musicale in Milan; by the *Corpus Scriptorum de Musica,* begun as recently as 1950, the editor of the first volumes of this excellent series being Joseph Smits van Waesberghe; and by the *Documenta Musicologica,* which the Bärenreiter Verlag of Kassel and Basel has published, in facsimile form, under the editorship of Hans Albrecht. If the *Antiquae Musicae Auctores Septem* of Meibom, the *Scriptores* of Gerbert, and the similar series by Coussemaker do not consistently measure up to present-day requirements, these old companions would nevertheless continue to provide help in abundance. And— as we are reminded merely by such names as those of Karl von Jan, Ingemar Düring, and Simon Cserba, among many others—the above-mentioned publications do not nearly exhaust the list of possible aids. It seems clear that the launching of the suggested project would not encounter insuperable obstacles. If it may be too much to hope for an equivalent of the Loeb Classical Library, whose regular format includes publication of texts in both the original language and English translation, perhaps a like plan could be followed only in those cases in which no acceptable edition of an original already exists. There seems to be no reason why absolute uniformity of method would have to be maintained throughout.

Whether or not a series of translations of the kind under discussion ever comes into being, it is hoped that the present assemblage of a fairly substantial number of summaries into a single brochure will in itself prove a convenient and useful implement for students, and also that as "finding tools" the sketches will help to lead investigators to sources containing, *in extenso,* basic information relevant to the subject of their study. Similar summaries of one item or another may, of course, be found in scattered places, but the compiler does not believe that the content gathered here closely resembles, as a whole, anything available elsewhere.

It is obvious that many qualified persons might well have preferred a selection of writings differing in certain respects from this one. Because the booklet is intended to stimulate the preparation of additional translations, writings originally in English are naturally not included, nor are works of which there are full and competently prepared English translations, if these are to be found in normal published form. (In a few instances, however, works have been admitted to this selection if such translations exist but have not been so published.) For the same reason, it has not been considered a prime desideratum to produce a series of summaries that is self-sufficient, well rounded, or balanced from the chronological standpoint. Since what has been denied or given a place within this booklet has been determined in part by what is or is not accessible in printed translation, the sketches deal with very little 19th-century material, this having already received considerable attention from a good number of assiduous translators. But medieval and Renaissance sources are represented to a much more liberal extent. Non-Western music is undoubtedly entitled to a fuller survey. The few items included here are intended as a reminder of the riches available rather than as an adequate representation. In this connection it should be mentioned that the summaries of material originally in Sanskrit and Arabic were made from publications in more familiar languages.

I am indebted to Professor Tatsuo Minagawa, of the Tokyo University of Arts, for selecting and summarizing the *Fūsi-Kaden* of Se-ami Motokiyo, and to Mr. Joseph Yasser for similar assistance in relation to the *Drevniaya Indo-Kitaiskaya Gamma v Asyi i Evrope* of Famintsin. Dr. Luther Dittmer and Dr. Robert Stevenson helped me most generously in bringing certain aspects of the work on this brochure to a conclusion, as did Dr. Catherine V. Brooks, Miss Liselotte Schmidt, Mr. Alexander Main, Mr. George Schuetze, Mr. Hans Lenneberg, and Mr. Ronald Cross—past or present students of mine in the Graduate School of Arts and Science at New York University.

GUSTAVE REESE

NOTE: What forms to adopt for proper names of early authors is a question for which no consistent answer has been attempted. The aim has simply been to use the forms most commonly employed by modern writers in English. For example, "Johannes de Grocheo," the Latin name of the Frenchman who was probably called "Jean de Grouchy," is more frequently encountered in English than the French name; on the other hand, the Italian "Guido d'Arezzo" designates the great 11th-century theorist more often in English than does the Latin "Guido Aretinus"; and still a third procedure—applying an Anglicized name—has become more or less standard with regard to Jerome of Moravia.

G. R.

KEY TO ABBREVIATIONS

Acta   *Acta Musicologica, Quarterly Magazine of the International Musicological Society.* 1928- .

AfMW   *Archiv für Musikwissenschaft.* Oct. 1918- Sept. 1927; revived 1952.

Apel, *Notation*   W. Apel. *The Notation of Polyphonic Music, 900-1600.* 4th ed., 1953.

BIMG   *Beihefte der Internationalen Musikgesellschaft.* 1. Folge, 1901-03; 2. Folge, 1905-14.

Coussemaker, *Moyen-Age*   C. E. H. Coussemaker. *Histoire de l'harmonie au moyen-âge.* 1852.

Coussemaker, *Scriptores*   C. E. H. Coussemaker. *Scriptorum de musica medii aevi nova series.* 4 vols., 1864-76; facs. ed., 1931.

CSM   *Corpus scriptorum de musica.* 1950- .

EC   *Encyclopédie de la musique et Dictionnaire du Conservatoire.* Ed. by A. Lavignac and L. de la Laurencie. *Partie I* in 5 vols.; *Partie II* in 6 vols. 1913-31.

Gerbert, *Scriptores*   M. Gerbert. *Scriptores ecclesiastici de musica.* 3 vols., 1784; facs. ed., 1931.

JAMS   *Journal of the American Musicological Society.* 1948- .

KJ   *Kirchenmusikalisches Jahrbuch.* 1886- .

M&L   *Music & Letters,* 1920- .

MD   *Musica disciplina.* 1948- .

MfMG   *Monatshefte für Musikgeschichte.* 1869-1905.

MGG   *Die Musik in Geschichte und Gegenwart.* Ed. by F. Blume. 1949- .

Migne, *Patrologia* (Greek)   J. P. Migne. *Patrologiae cursus completus. Series Graeca.* 166 vols., 1857-66.

Migne, *Patro-logia* (Latin)	J. P. Migne. *Patrologiae cursus completus. Series Latina.* 221 vols., 1844-55.
MQ	*The Musical Quarterly.* 1915- .
PAPTM	*Publikation älterer praktischer und theoretischer Musikwerke.* Ed. by R. Eitner. 29 vols., 1873-1905.
Reese, *Middle Ages*	G. Reese. *Music in the Middle Ages.* 1940.
Reese, *Renaissance*	G. Reese. *Music in the Renaissance.* 1954.
Riemann, *Musiktheorie*	H. Riemann. *Geschichte der Musiktheorie im IX.-XIX. Jahrhundert.* 2nd. ed., 1921.
SIMG	*Sammelbände der Internationalen Musikgesellschaft.* Oct. 1899-Sept. 1914.
Strunk, *Source Readings*	O. Strunk. *Source Readings in Music History.* 1950.
VfMW	*Vierteljahrsschrift für Musikwissenschaft.* 1884-94.
ZfMW	*Zeitschrift für Musikwissenschaft.* 1918-35.

Fourscore Classics
of Music Literature

GREEK ANTIQUITY AND BYZANTIUM

1

PTOLEMY (CLAUDIUS PTOLEMAEUS). *Harmonikd.* 2nd century.

Ptolemy, the famous Greco-Egyptian astronomer, mathematician, and geographer, has left us "the most scientific and best arranged treatise on the theory of musical scales that we possess in Greek." There are three books, each containing sixteen chapters. Books I and II deal with tuning, intervals, scales, the three genera (diatonic, chromatic, and enharmonic, the last of these, however, being mentioned as no longer in use), the Greater Perfect System (two-octave gamut, having the basic structure of a modern two-octave scale on A without sharps or flats, but transposable), and the use of the monochord. In addition to offering his own ratios for the various intervals, Ptolemy reviews the ratios given by Archytas (400 B.C.), Aristoxenus (300 B.C.), Eratosthenes (240 B.C.), and Didymus (A.D. 60). The *tonoi* are treated not as key transpositions of the gamut intact, as with the Aristoxenians, but as key transpositions which, in each instance, bring within a stationary medium compass (practical with regard to the limitations of voices and instruments) a different octave species or segment of the gamut, i.e., a different sequence of tones and semitones (also, in the enharmonic genus, smaller intervals). Book III (which may not be by Ptolemy) speculates on relations between music and the human soul and between music and celestial phenomena. In addition to discussing the music of his own time, Ptolemy reviews the much earlier Pythagorean and Aristoxenian systems. He advocates a compromise between the mathematical principles of the former and the reliance of the latter on aural judgment. One of his tunings, the syntonic diatonic, is equivalent to modern "just" intonation. The *Harmoniká* was drawn upon by Boethius and other medieval writers. Thus, in addition to being a main source for our knowledge of ancient Greek music, it provides valuable aid to the understanding of Western medieval theory.

With Latin tr. and commentary by John Wallis, *Claudii Ptolemaei harmonicorum libri III* (1682); in Greek only by Ingemar Düring, *Die Harmonielehre des Klaudios Ptolemaios* (1930); German tr. and commentary by I. Düring in *Ptolemaios und Porphyrios über die Musik* (1934). See also Sir Francis Haskins Eyles Stiles, "An Explanation of the Modes or Tones in the Ancient Greek Music," in *Philosophical Transactions of the Royal Society of London*, LI (1760), 695; J. F. Mountford, "The Harmonics of Ptolemy and the Lacuna in 11. 14," in *Transactions of the American Philological Association*, LVII (1926), 71 (from which the quotation at the opening of the above sketch is taken); Otto Gombosi, *Tonarten und Stimmungen der antiken Musik* (1939), *passim;* Reese, *Middle Ages,* ch. 2.

2

ARISTIDES QUINTILIANUS. *Peri mousikes (De musica).* 2nd or 3rd century.

This treatise, encyclopedic in scope, is divided into three books. The first, after comments on the moral value of music, deals, much in the spirit of Aristoxenus, with harmony in the Greek sense (i.e., with the study of melodic sounds and intervals) and provides (the only source to do so, in spite of the author's late date) some precise information regarding the six harmoniai referred to in Plato's *Republic.* Discussion of rhythm and meter follows. Book II, devoted to the role of music in education, is much influenced by

Plato (Cicero is drawn upon also) and includes discussion of ethos, i.e., of the effect of the art on character and on the emotions. The fullness and chronological range of this discussion make Book II one of our main sources of knowledge concerning the musical aesthetics of antiquity. In Book III, the author turns to the relations between music and nature and treats of such matters as number symbolism, parallels between phenomena in the cosmos and in music, etc. If Book I sheds light on the history of music, Books II and III cast it more on the connections between this history and that of ideas.

In Marcus Meibom, *Antiquae musicae auctores septem*, II (1652); A. Jahn, *Aristidis Quintiliani de musica libri III* (1882); German tr. in R. Schäfke, *Aristeides Quintilianus, Von der Musik* (1937). See also C. E. Ruelle, "Le Musicographe Aristide Quintilien," *SIMG*, XI (1910), 313; W. Vetter in *MGG*, I, 629 ff. (including lengthy bibliography).

3

CONSTANTINE VII (CONSTANTINE PORPHYROGENITUS). *Syntagma*, usually referred to by the Latin title, *De caeremoniis aulae byzantinae*. Circa 940-959.

This descriptive account of the ceremonies of the Byzantine court is one of a number of works written or inspired by the Eastern Roman emperor that provide information concerning Byzantine military and political affairs during and before Constantine's time. The *De caeremoniis* comprises two books. Book I, completed before Constantine rose to full authority in 944, is a detailed description of Eastern church and court ceremonial practices of the preceding 250 years. Book II, set down in the last year or so of Constantine's life, is a rather fragmentary piece of writing that includes chapters on such matters as military tactics and imperial finance, in addition to material supplementing

Book I. It is Book I, then, that is of real interest to the music scholar.

Constantine was a patron of the arts, and himself a painter and poet. Eleven of his texts are still used in the Greek Church today, and at least one modern scholar has suggested that some of the texts for music, transmitted by the *De caeremoniis* itself, may have been written by him. His interest in music is well established, and there is evidence suggesting that he had some competence as a musician. Thus his accounts of religious, civil, and secular ceremonies do not fail to mention the musical adornments to these occasions. Repeatedly one reads of singing by soloists, or by a choir, or by the assembled populace, and of the organs playing at the palace. Trumpets are mentioned, as well as a drum and a zither, but voices clearly dominate in the ceremonial music. Ninety-four texts for musical compositions are contained in the *De caeremoniis;* in many instances the reader is informed not only regarding the occasion for which a piece was intended, but also regarding its type and *echos* (mode). Since many of the ninety-four texts are mentioned in connection with more than one *echos,* the total number of pieces represented by them is considerably higher. The *De caeremoniis* is valuable not only as a source of fairly specific musicopoetical information but as a colorful depiction of the role of music in the public life of medieval Constantinople.

Edited with commentary by J. J. Reiske in *Corpus scriptorum historiae byzantinae,* IV [1,2] (1829-30); also in Migne, *Patrologia* (Greek), CXII (1864), 73. In part, with French tr. and commentary by A. Vogt, *Constantin VII Porphyrogénète, Le Livre des cérémonies,* 4 vols. (1935-40). See also Jacques Handschin, *Das Zeremonienwerk Kaiser Konstantins und die sangbare Dichtung* (1942).

ISLAM AND THE ORIENT

4

BHĀRATA. *Nāṭya-śāstra*. Conjectural datings range as widely as from the 4th century B.C. to the 5th century A.D.

Some of this vast, encyclopedic book on the theatrical arts of ancient India constitutes the oldest and most important treatise on early Indian music. The older sources divide the contents into thirty-six chapters. Chapters 4 and 5, although dealing mainly with religious observances, provide valuable information on music and the dance. Chapters 28-33 are specifically devoted to music. There is a discussion of vocal music that gives rules for performing the ten types of Indian song, explains the four ways of fitting text and melody together, and has information on ornamentation and other related topics. The extensive sections on instrumental music describe wind and string instruments, discuss types of instrumental composition (with examples), present methods of performance and information on ornamentation, and classify various kinds of instrumental music by tone color. The theory of music in ancient India is given considerable attention. Included are descriptions of the twenty-two *śrutis* (small intervals) that make up the octave and of the two *grāmas* (basic scales), as well as of rhythm. Binary and ternary meter and means of beating the measure are investigated.

Sanskrit text, with commentary by Abhinavagupta (11th century) and English preface, appendix, and index, ed. by Manalli Ramakrishna Kavi, 2 vols. of a projected 4, containing 18 chs. (1926-34); another ed. by Joanny Grosset, *Traité de Bharata sur le théâtre, texte sanscrit, édition critique*, Vol. I of a projected 3 vols., containing 14 chs.

(Fasc. XL of the *Annales de l'Université de Lyon,* 1898); English tr. of ch. 4, with a glossary of technical dance terms from chs. 8-11, in *Taṇḍava Lakṣaṇam; or The Fundamentals of Ancient Hindu Dancing,* by Bijayeti Venkata Narayanaswami Naidu and others (1936). See also the following (several of which contain extracts in tr.): Joanny Grosset, "Contribution à l'étude de la musique hindou," *Bibliothèque de la Faculté des Lettres de Lyon,* VII (1888), and "Inde," in *EC,* Pt. I, Vol. I, pp. 257 ff.; E. Clements, *Introduction to the Study of Indian Music* (1913); Bernhard Breloer, *Die Grundelemente der altindischen Musik nach dem Bhāratīya-naṭya-śāstra* (1922); Curt Sachs, *The Rise of Music in the Ancient World East and West* (1943).

5

AL-KINDĪ, ABŪ YŪSUF, YAʻQŪB IBN ISHĀQ. *Risāla fī khubr taʼlīf al-alḥān.* 9th century.

This *Treatise on the Inner Knowledge of the Composition of Melodies* is among the earliest surviving writings in Arabic on the subject of music. It is largely concerned with Greek doctrine, but some of it, e.g., the portions dealing with the lute, are independent of Greek sources. The *Risāla* treats of the tuning of the lute, the number and function of the notes (their position within the double octave, the two species of double octave, fixed and variable notes, the names of the tetrachords and their notes, etc.), the seven modes, transitions (from note to note, interval to interval, genus to genus, unit to unit, mode to mode), ethos, composition (this section gives more details regarding melodic structures in Greek *melopoiia* than do the known Greek sources), and music and prosody. The decisive influence of Greek thought on the Orient toward the end of the first millenium A.D. is clearly shown.

With German tr. in R. Lachmann and Mahmud el-Hefni,

Ja 'qūb Ibn Ishāq al-Kindī Risāla . . . (1931). See also H. G. Farmer, *History of Arabian Music* (1929) and *Sources of Arabian Music* (1940).

6

AL-FĀRĀBĪ, ABŪ NAṢR, MUḤAMMAD IBN MUḤAMMAD IBN TARKHĀN. *Kitāb al-mūsīqī al-kabīr.* 10th century.

The Arabic philosopher Al-Fārābī (*c.* 870-*c.* 950) was a skilled lutenist. Thus his several works on music combine the authority of the trained musical performer with that of the systematic theorist. The most important of these works is the *Kitāb al-mūsīqī al-kabīr* (*Great Book on Music*), which has been admired by leading Arabic, Persian, Turkish, and Indian musical writers from the 11th to the 20th centuries. Based upon Greek musical theory, better known in the Near East than in Europe during the Middle Ages, the *Kitāb* was a key work in the development of the Arabic musical system. Although the Greek tradition influenced both the Arabic and the European musical systems, the two were to evolve in separate directions.

The *Kitāb* originally comprised two volumes; the second, a review of earlier theories, has not been preserved. The surviving volume, consisting of a lengthy introduction and three Books, is a systematic treatment of music according to Al-Fārābī's own views. The introduction deals with a number of fundamental matters, including the various genera, consonance and dissonance, and the psychological effects of different kinds of music. Book I discusses the physical and mathematical bases of music, and describes in detail the complex Arabic system of scales and genera. Rhythm is discussed far more clearly and precisely than in any known European treatise written before the 13th century. Book II contains a detailed treatment of lute tuning and technique, and shorter discussions of other important

Arabic instruments, including flutes and harps. Book III, devoted to instrumental and vocal composition, includes valuable material on traditional Arabic rhythmic patterns. Written by a distinguished musician and great scholar, the *Kitāb* is an essential source of information concerning the rich musical culture of medieval Islam.

Extracts ed. by J. G. L. Kosegarten in *Alii Ispahanensis liber cantilenarum magnus* (1840-43), and in *Zeitschrift für die Kunde des Morgenlandes,* V (1844), 151 ff. Most of the text dealing with instruments ed. by J. P. N. Land in *Actes du Sixième Congrès international des Orientalistes* (1883), Pt. I, pp. 133 ff., and in *Recherches sur l'histoire de la gamme arabe* (1884). Complete French tr. in Rodolphe d'Erlanger, *La Musique arabe,* I (1930), II (1935). Extracts in Latin and German tr. in Kosegarten, *op. cit.* Extracts in Spanish tr. (unreliable) by M. Soriano-Fuertes in *Música Arabe-Española* (1853). Extracts in French tr. in Land, *op. cit.,* pp. 100 ff. Extracts in Dutch tr. in Land, *Over de Toonladders der Arabische Muziek* (1880). See also Henry George Farmer, *A History of Arabian Music* (1929), pp. 175 ff.

7

Se-ami Motokiyo. *Fūsi-Kaden,* more commonly called *Kadénsho.* Circa 1400.

This *Book of the Secret Principles of "Hana"* is on the aesthetics and practice of the Nō-play, a type of Japanese classic drama. (Like ancient Greek drama, this is a composite of music—for solo voices, chorus, and instruments—and poetry, drama, and dance.) Se-ami, who with his father, Kwannami Kiyotsugu, initiated the Nō-play, was a composer, librettist, choreographer, actor, and producer, and also wrote between twenty and twenty-five theoretical works on the subject. Among these the *Fūsi-Kaden* is the most important and is, indeed, fundamental. The book is divided into an introduction and seven chapters. In the introduction Se-ami gives an outline of the history of the Nō and the rules governing the players. In chapter 1, he tells how the actors should practice and study the art of the Nō—including singing—at various ages. In chapter 2, Se-ami takes up the proper manner of expressing and representing the characteristics of a role; he also discusses the relation between realism and symbolism with reference to the special characteristics of certain types of roles, e.g., old men, madmen, supernatural beings, and women (who were played by masked men). Chapter 3 is concerned with how to produce a deep dramatic and musical impression on audiences, and how to win Nō contests. Chapter 4 is again about the history of the Nō, and chapter 5 sets forth the qualities that will enable the singing actor to appeal to audiences made up of people with varying degrees of intelligence and sensibility. In chapter 6, methods of composing the text and music of Nō-plays are described, and the three basic aesthetic principles of Nō are discussed. These are *Yūgen* (elegance and profundity), *Mono-mane* (realism), and *Hana* ("flower," i.e., the power to captivate an audience). In chapter 7, Se-ami explains these principles in detail. The *Fūsi-Kaden,* like other books by Se-ami, goes beyond its primary usefulness to Nō-players, and provides much information for musicians, actors, dancers, composers, and librettists generally. The place of his books in oriental literature might well be likened to that of Wagner's essays on the *Gesamtkunst* in Western culture.

Editions in classical Japanese: *Se-ami Jūrokubu Hyōsyaku,* ed. by Tomotsugu Nose (1940); *Kōchū Kadénsho,* ed. by Ichima Kawase (1954). In modern Japanese, *Se-ami Jūrokubu Shu,* ed. by Jinichi Konishi (1954).

THE MIDDLE AGES IN EUROPE

8

BOETHIUS. *De institutione musica.* 6th century.

Medieval respect for *auctoritas* made this work possibly the most influential treatise in the history of music. This explains the numerous copies that exist. In 1492, almost a thousand years after it was written, the treatise remained important enough to be printed while printing was still in its infancy. The work is not primarily one of great originality, discussing as it does the theories of Pythagoras, Nicomachus, Aristoxenus, and Ptolemy. These, however, are not merely restated but are juxtaposed, analyzed, and explained. Although the title he uses seems to embrace the entire field of music, Boethius discusses neither rhythm nor melody; aside from philosophical matters, he deals only with problems of harmony (in the ancient sense) and of acoustics. Of interest in his philosophy is the division of music into *musica mundana* (the music implied in the orderly movement of the heavenly bodies), *musica humana* (which likens the harmonious relation between soul and body to musical consonance), and *musica instrumentalis* (music proper). To Boethius, as shown by him outside this treatise, music is part of the *quadrivium* (together with arithmetic, geometry, and astronomy) rather than of the *trivium* (consisting of grammar, rhetoric, and logic).

The treatise is organized somewhat like a textbook, progressing, in Book I, from simpler questions of acoustics and harmony to more complex problems relating to the same subjects. Books II and III present and discuss theories of Pythagoras and Aristoxenus. In Book III Boethius employs the Latin letters A through P in a diagram to represent the degrees of a double octave. The musical notation using these letters, found in some 10th- and 11th-century manuscripts, has consequently been called Boethian. Whether Boethius himself, however, intended the letters as a means of notation or only as a means of exposition has been questioned. If he intended them in the former sense (which seems possible), there is some historical significance in the application of Latin letters, rather than Greek ones (as in antiquity), to represent notes. In Book IV, intervals are related to the monochord. Book V is devoted to Ptolemy and his tonal system. Here Boethius uses the Latin term *modus* in translating the Greek word *tonos*. This later led medieval musicians into the error of designating the ecclesiastical modes, not by the names of their nearest equivalents in the Greek system, but by the names of the Greek keys—a custom still followed today.

For a complete list of early printings see R. Wagner in *MGG*, II, 49 ff. Modern ed. by Gottfried Friedlein (1847); a new ed. by Roger Bragard is planned; German tr. by Oskar Paul (1872). See also R. Bragard, "L'Harmonie des Sphères selon Boèce," *Speculum,* IV (1929), 206; Leo Schrade, "Music in the Philosophy of Boethius," *MQ,* XXXIII (1947), 188; A. J. H. Vincent, "De la Notation musicale attribuée à Boèce," *Le Correspondant (Religion, . . . Littérature, Beaux-Arts),* XXXVI (1855), 366; Curt Sachs, *The Rise of Music in the Ancient World East and West* (1943); Reese, *Middle Ages.*

9

ANONYMOUS. *Musica Enchiriadis.* (Formerly misattributed to Hucbald; perhaps by Otgerus, Count of Laon and Abbot of St. Amand; the title is a corruption of *Enchiridion de Musica,** "Manual on Music.") Late 9th century.

* *Enchiridion* is corrupted into *Enchirias,* and the latter (treated as the name of a person) is turned into the genitive case.

This treatise and the contemporary *Scholia* on it include information regarding organum as it was practiced in the 9th century and, in doing so, are the oldest theoretical sources that give us precise data concerning early part-music. The *Musica Enchiriadis* is made up of nineteen chapters, whose contents may be briefly indicated as follows: (1) the gamut and its tetrachordal structure; (2) the notation (in a type known as Daseian) of the gamut; (3) the *finalis* (i.e., D, E, F, or G) in each of the four authentic-plagal modal pairs; (4) the ambitus of the four modal pairs expressed in relation to the *finalis;* (5) the difference between authentic and plagal modes; (6) how to sing musical intervals; (7) a musical exercise demonstrating the notes; (8) further musical examples in several modes; (9) definitions of various terms; (10) the symphonies of the fourth, fifth, and octave ("symphony is the sweet agreement of different sounds joined together"); (11) symphonies of the eleventh, twelfth, and double octave; (12) the same continued; (13) discussion of a musical organization, organum, in which there is movement of sounds according to one symphony, e.g., in parallel fourths; (14) the same style of organum in parallel fourths expanded to four voices; (15) organum by parallel fifths; (16) references to Ptolemy and Boethius; (17) organum that begins at the unison and opens out into parallel fourths; (18) the use of intervals smaller than the fourth in the course of an organum; (19) the effect of music on the mind and soul.

The set of *Scholia* provides a commentary on the "Manual" and consists of a dialogue—a pupil's questions and his teacher's answers. It is in three parts presenting: (1) the elements of music (including a discussion of the singing of chant); (2) more about symphonies; (3) mathematical proportions.

In Gerbert, *Scriptores,* I, 152 (*Scholia, ibid.,* p. 173); also Migne, *Patrologia* (Latin), CXXXII (1853), 957 (*Scholia, ibid.,* p. 981). German tr. (incl. *Scholia* and comments) in Raimund Schlecht, "Musica Enchiriadis von Hucbald,"

MfMG, VI (1874), 163, 179; VII (1875), 1, 17, 33, 49, 65, 81; VIII (1876), 89. English tr. of a portion of the *Scholia* in Strunk, *Source Readings,* pp. 126 ff. See also Heinrich Sowa, "Textvarianten zur Musica Enchiriadis," *ZfMW,* XVII (1935), 194; Philipp Spitta, "Die Musica Enchiriadis und ihr Zeitalter," *VfMW,* V (1889), 443; Joseph Smits van Waesberghe, "La Place exceptionelle de l'Ars Musica dans le développement des sciences au siècle des Carolingiens," *Revue Grégorienne,* XXXI (1952), 81; A. H. Fox Strangways, "A Tenth Century Manual," *M&L,* XIII (1932), 183; and E. J. Grutchfield, "Hucbald: A Millenary Commemoration," *Musical Times,* LXXI (1930), 507, 704.

10

GUIDO D'AREZZO. *Micrologus.* Early 11th century.

The *Micrologus* is the most extensive of Guido d'Arezzo's valuable writings. Among the subjects dealt with in its twenty chapters are the gamut, the disposition of the notes on the monochord, tones and semitones, intervals, the church modes, intervallic relationships, transposition, tropes and ethos, how to compose a good melody, neumes, improvisation, and organum. In his chapter on organum Guido gives preference to the free (i.e., not strictly parallel) forms; while organum at the fourth is described, organum at the fifth is no longer allowed, and no interval larger than a fourth is permitted between the *vox principalis* and *vox organalis.* Minor seconds are forbidden. Much attention is paid to the cadence group (*occursus*), where oblique motion is introduced, as well as some contrary motion and voice-crossing.

In Gerbert, *Scriptores,* II, 2; Migne, *Patrologia* (Latin), CXLI (1853), 379; Ambrosio M. Amelli (ed.), *Guidonis Monachi Aretini, Micrologus ad praestantiones codices mss. exactus* (1904); Joseph Smits van Waesberghe (ed.), in CSM,

IV (1955). German tr. in Michael Hermesdorff, *Micrologus Guidonis de disciplina artis musicae, d.i. Kurze Abhandlung Guidos über die Regeln der musikalischen Kunst* (1876). French tr. of many passages in Louis Lambillote, *Esthétique, théorie et pratique du chant grégorien* (1855). See also Hans Oesch, *Guido von Arezzo; Biographisches und Theoretisches unter besonderer Berücksichtigung der sogenannten odonischen Traktate (Publikationen der Schweizerischen musikforschenden Gesellschaft*, Ser. 2, Vol. IV, 1956); Joseph Smits van Waesberghe, *De musico-paedagogico et theoretico Guidone Aretino* (1953); English tr. of two chapters of the latter item as articles, "The Musical Notation of Guido of Arezzo" and "Guido of Arezzo and Musical Improvisation" in *MD*, V (1951), 15, 55.

11

RUDOLPH OF ST. TROND (?). *Quaestiones in musica.* Circa 1100.

Apparently written in connection with the putative author's pedagogical and scholarly activities at the monastery of St. Trond, in Liège, the *Quaestiones* is an extensive treatise on church music. The author deals with both practical and speculative matters, and he shows a wide knowledge of earlier writers from Boethius to Guido d'Arezzo and other 11th-century figures. Thus, although the *Quaestiones* presents little that is original, it is a valuable summary of medieval musical thought and practice.

The work is divided into two main sections, each containing twenty-seven questions or chapters. Section I deals with purely musical subjects, including scales, tetrachords, intervals, the modes, vocal performance, bells, and organ pipes. Most of Section II is devoted to the relationship between music and arithmetic, reflecting the inclusion of music in the medieval *quadrivium* of the liberal disciplines; arithmetic is here regarded as "the mother of music." Much of this material is drawn from the *Scholia Enchiriadis,* but is more clearly presented in the *Quaestiones.* The final four chapters properly belong to Section I, as they treat practical matters like tuning and the modes. The last chapter demonstrates the pre-Guidonian use of a horizontal line and a capital letter (clef) to define the pitch of a melody notated in staffless neumes. Throughout the *Quaestiones* there is considerable use of verse and diagrams as instructional aids.

With commentary in Rudolf Steglich, *Die Quaestiones in Musica, BIMG,* 2. Folge, X (1911). For bibliographical and other information see also Joseph Smits van Waesberghe, *Muziekgeschiedenis der Middeleeuwen,* I (1936-39), 225.

12

JOHANNES AFFLIGEMENSIS. *De musica.* (Formerly incorrectly attributed to John Cotton.) Circa 1100.

This treatise is concerned with the usual topics of medieval musical speculation and practical musical theory: the establishment of music as a scholarly discipline alongside its practice as an art, definitions and classifications of music, its inventors, musical instruments, the divisions of the monochord, proportions, the ecclesiastical modes, the psalm tones, Greek notational theory, rules for composing songs, and diaphony. Diaphony, which the author indicates (in the historically most informative section of the treatise) is commonly called organum, utilizes the unison, fourth, fifth, and octave indiscriminately and permits the crossing of voices, the result being that contrary motion of the voice parts becomes preferred to parallel motion. As in Guido d'Arezzo, ethical connotations are attributed to the ecclesiastical modes.

In Gerbert, *Scriptores,* II, 230; Joseph Smits van Waesberghe (ed.), in *CSM*, I (1950). German tr. in Utto Korn-müller, "Der Traktat des Johannes Cottonis über Musik," *KJ*, XIII (1888), 1. See also Joseph Smits van Waesberghe, "Some Music Treatises and their Interrelation," *MD*, III (1949), 25, 95, and "John of Affligem or John Cotton?" *MD*, VI (1952), 139.

13

ANONYMOUS. *Ad organum faciendum.* Late 11th or early 12th century.

This work makes available valuable information concerning organum as well as examples of it. It thus resembles the treatise of Johannes Affligemensis, but the author, apparently a Frenchman, approaches the subject of organum with greater enthusiasm. The first part of the treatise, written in prose, groups various organum combinations into "modes" or types. In this section occur the earliest examples (in a theoretical work) in which the *vox principalis* is placed below the *vox organalis*. It is of historical interest that the author flattens *b* in his musical examples to avoid the augmented fourth as a harmonic interval, whereas in earlier writing it was the custom to avoid that interval by keeping the lower voice stationary. The same melody reappears in the *vox principalis* of several examples, each time with a different *vox organalis,* a point of interest in the history of the theory of counterpoint. The second part of the treatise, written in verse, gives additional rules and examples and ends with a panegyric in which the author extols organum above plainsong.

In Coussemaker, *Moyen-Age,* p. 229 (with a parallel French tr.). See also Riemann, *Musiktheorie,* pp. 85 ff.; Erich Steinhard, "Zur Frühgeschichte der Mehrstimmigkeit," *AfMW*, III (1921), 224; *Oxford History of Music*, I (1929), 37 ff.

14

ANONYMOUS. *Discantus positio vulgaris.* Circa 1220-1230.

This short treatise survives as Jerome of Moravia incorporated it in the twenty-sixth chapter of his *Tractatus de musica.* It is the earliest extant treatise dealing with mensural notation. Moreover, in its discussion of the style of motet composition, it differs from theoretical writings of the period in its exclusive concentration upon that style as represented in documents earlier than the added fascicles of the Montpellier manuscript. Although the introduction of mensural notation portended the gradual breakdown of the framework of the rhythmic modes, this treatise alone recognizes none of the factors that caused the final disintegration of those modes: equivalence, division of the mode, irregular modes, etc. Mensural principles are applied only to single notes, whereas ligatures can be made mensural only by widening the first head of a two-note ligature. The fifth and the octave are recognized as the best consonances and are recommended for alternating (i.e., accented) beats; the proper voice-leading of each of two parts between consonances is expounded in detail. The polyphonic musical forms which the author lists are two varieties of organum (pure and duplex), the motet, the conductus, and the hocket.

In Coussemaker, *Scriptores,* I, 94; Simon M. Cserba, *Hieronymus de Moravia (Freiburger Studien zur Musikwissenschaft,* Heft 2, 1935), p. 189. In part, with parallel French tr., in Coussemaker, *Moyen-Age,* pp. 247 ff. See also Reese, *Middle Ages.*

15

JOHANNES DE GARLANDIA (THE ELDER). *De musica mensurabili positio.* Circa 1240-1250.

This treatise on early mensural music is most informative because of its inclusion of copious documentation in the form of notated musical examples for the various rules adduced by the author. The treatise is mainly concerned with the notation of the rhythmic modes in ligatures and the combination of these modes in different voices of the same composition. The nature of the consonances and the problem of *musica ficta* provide further topics of discussion.

In the version incorporated in Jerome of Moravia's *Tractatus de musica,* in Coussemaker, *Scriptores,* I, 97, and in Simon M. Cserba, *Hieronymus de Moravia (Freiburger Studien zur Musikwissenschaft,* Heft 2, 1935), p. 195. According to the version of the Vatican MS, in Coussemaker, *Scriptores,* I, 175.

16

ANONYMUS IV. *De mensuris et discantu.* Circa 1270.

The treatise of the fourth anonymous author in Coussemaker's *Scriptores,* Vol. I, commonly regarded as actually consisting of the notes of an English student in Paris, provides us with the most important historical data concerning polyphonic music performed at the Cathedral of Notre Dame in Paris during the time in which the present edifice was being constructed. The significant contributions of the two great composers whose names have come down to us, Leoninus and Perotinus, are discussed in less ambiguous terms than in any other treatise; moreover, the *Magnus liber,* attributed to Leoninus, is described in sufficient detail to enable us to identify the contents of this volume in several surviving manuscripts. Although the main practical value of this treatise lies in the systematic discussion of the notation of the modes in ligatures, the references to other musical centers, primarily in England, is of the greatest importance; we learn of "good singers" like John filius Dei, Makeblith in Winchester, and Blakesmith at the court of Henry III; the Worcester musical tradition is connected with the "Homines occidentales" and the "Westcuntre."

In Coussemaker, *Scriptores*, I, 327. See also Walter Niemann, "Über die abweichende Bedeutung der Ligaturen in der Mensuraltheorie der Zeit vor Johannes de Garlandia," *BIMG*, 1. Folge, VI (1902); Johannes Wolf, "Early English Musical Theorists," *MQ*, XXIX (1939), 420; Luther Dittmer, "Binary Rhythm, Musical Theory and the Worcester Fragments," *MD*, VII (1953), 39; William Waite, *The Rhythm of Twelfth-Century Polyphony* (1954); and Reese, *Middle Ages*.

17

JEROME OF MORAVIA. *Tractatus de musica*. Second half of the 13th century.

The treatise of Jerome of Moravia, a Dominican music professor at St. Jacques in Paris, is a compilation of the important musical speculation and practical musical theory of the time. Jerome himself makes no noteworthy contribution to musical speculation but draws freely upon Boethius, Isidore of Seville, Al-Fārābī, Guido d'Arezzo, Johannes Affligemensis, and a host of others. On the outstanding question of mensural music, Jerome also takes no independent stand but does incorporate four important treatises into his twenty-sixth chapter: *Discantus positio vulgaris*, *De musica mensurabili positio* (Johannes de Garlandia), *Ars cantus mensurabilis* (Franco of Cologne), and *Musica mensurabilis* (Petrus Picardus). Valuable as are his restatements of discussions regarding mutations (ch. 12), consonances (ch. 15), carillons (ch. 18), divisions of the monochord (ch. 19), and the ecclesiastical modes (chs. 20-22), the chief contributions of this treatise are Jerome's own original sections detailing certain aspects of the practical music of the time. In chapter 28 Jerome, like Johannes de Grocheo, discusses musical instruments, especially the viol (viella)—for which he gives three tunings—and the rubebe. In chapter 25 he provides some fairly definite rules for a rhythmic interpretation of plainsong. Jerome mentions the office of the precentor, but does not define the method by which he conducts.

In Coussemaker, *Scriptores,* I, 1; Leo Liepmannssohn, *Tractatus de musica compilatus a fratre Jeronimo Moravo ordinis fratrum predicatorum* (1899); and Simon M. Cserba, *Hieronymus de Moravia (Freiburger Studien zur Musikwissenschaft,* Heft 2, 1935). See also Utto Kornmüller, "Die alten Musiktheoretiker," *KJ,* XIV (1889), 1, and Reese, *Middle Ages.*

18

WALTER ODINGTON. *De speculatione musicae.* Circa 1300.

Although Odington, an Englishman writing in Evesham Abbey near Worcester, devotes much space to the usual topics of medieval musical treatises—notably the mathematical proportions of sounds, Greek musical theory, the divisions of the monochord, metrics, and the ecclesiastical modes—the last of the six parts of this treatise, dealing with polyphonic music, is by far the most significant and informative. Even though of limited value as an aid in interpreting the music of Notre Dame Cathedral itself, because much later than most other treatises of this period and because it comes from a peripheral area, this document is highly important by reason of its discussion of music in England prior to the exclusive adoption of French musical style, notation, and rhythm. Odington's close relationship to the Worcester circle makes him the chief theorist for the interpretation of its music; his descriptions of the rondellus, the hocket, and the conductus are much more applicable to English compositions than to French, whereas those of the motets, organa, and copulae appear to be more in keeping with the French tradition. An interesting detail mentioned by Odington is the fact that when the tenor has long sustained notes they should be sung *tremolando*.

In Coussemaker, *Scriptores*, I, 182. See also Luther Dittmer, "Binary Rhythm, Musical Theory and the Worcester Fragments," *MD*, VII (1953), 39.

19

JOHANNES DE GROCHEO. *Theoria* (the title of J. Wolf's edition, the original being without title), or *De musica* (the title of E. Rohloff's edition). Circa 1300.

This treatise is unique in its time; it departs from tradition by emphasizing not the wisdom of ancient writers but rather the contemporary musical scene in Paris. It is unrivaled as a source of information on secular music before 1300. The main body of the treatise is devoted to descriptions of musical forms and includes many references to performance practice; this main body is preceded by a discussion of consonances and intervals. Grocheo rejects the old division of music into *musica mundana, musica humana,* and *musica instrumentalis* (cf. Boethius)—also the division, more usual for his time, into *musica mensurabilis* and *musica immensurabilis*—and classifies the music of his own day into three principal groups: (1) *musica vulgaris,* the simple, monophonic music of the common people; (2) *musica mensurabilis,* the measured, polyphonic music cultivated by educated society; and (3) *musica ecclesiastica,* music for the church, which combines elements of the first two groups. An explanation of the gamut and solmization follows, after which Grocheo discusses the musical forms of each of his three groups. Under *musica vulgaris* he includes the *chanson de geste, stantipes, ductia,* and various other types; he differentiates between vocal and instrumental forms and praises the viol above other instruments, stating that it may be used to play all of the forms. He classifies measured music into the motet, organum, and hocket. He treats *musica ecclesiastica* briefly since, he explains, churches differ from one another in practice. The treatise ends with a discussion of some liturgical forms and an explanation of the church modes; the latter, he remarks, are of no consequence in secular music.

With a German tr. in Ernst Rohloff, *Der Musiktraktat des Johannes de Grocheo* (1943), an improvement upon J. Wolf's ed. in *SIMG,* I (1899), 69. See also Ernst Rohloff, *Studien zum Musiktraktat des Johannes de Grocheo* (1930); Riemann, *Musiktheorie,* pp. 207 ff.

20

Marchettus de Padua. *Pomerium.* Circa 1318.

This treatise, devoted to mensural notation—in particular to the system used by the Italians in the early 14th century—contains the first theoretical discussion of duple time as of equal rank with triple time. The work is evidence of the independence of the early Italian *trecento* system of notation from French *ars nova* theory. It also provides the clearest description we have of the transitional French notation of the same period. The treatise consists of three books. Book I, by far the longest, is mainly devoted to an extensive general treatment of rhythm and its notation. Book II discusses duple time and the differences between the Italian and French practices therein. Book III deals with ligatures.

In Gerbert, *Scriptores,* III, 121. An ed. by G. Vecchi has been announced for early publication in *CSM,* V. English tr. of Bk. II in Strunk, *Source Readings,* pp. 160 ff. See also Oliver Strunk, "Intorno a Marchetto da Padua," in *La Rassegna musicale,* XX (1950), 312; Nino Pirrotta, "Marchettus de Padua and the Italian Ars Nova," in *MD,* IX (1955), 57.

21

PHILIPPE DE VITRY. *Ars nova.* Circa 1320.

This famous work, apparently written in Paris, is the first treatise by a French musician to describe duple meter as of equal rank with triple meter. The *Ars nova* discusses intervals, the gamut, accidentals, and the system of hexachords and mutations. Philippe gives special attention to the semitone, for it is "the sweetness and spice of all song." A passage on *musica falsa (musica ficta)* includes the statement that the practice is "not false, but true and necessary, since no motet or *rondellus* can be sung without it."

But it is the latter part of the *Ars nova* that is really significant, for it presents a thorough explanation of both binary and ternary mensuration, and introduces a complete system of time signatures that was so novel as not to pass into general use before the end of the century. The principles of Philippe's mensural system, based on what came to be called "the four prolations" (equivalent, in a way, to our $\frac{9}{8}$, $\frac{3}{4}$, $\frac{6}{8}$, and $\frac{2}{4}$), remained in use well into the Renaissance. One of his time signatures, the C, has survived to the present day, albeit with a changed meaning. Also included in the *Ars nova* is a valuable account of red notation and its seven uses, one being to indicate a reduction of a time value by a third. This treatise, a practical, nonspeculative work by one of the leading musicians of the time, is among our prime sources of information concerning the music of 14th-century France.

In Coussemaker, *Scriptores,* III, 13. See Apel, *Notation,* pp. 338 ff.; Gilbert Reaney, "The 'Ars Nova' of Philippe de

Vitry," in *MD*, X (1956), 5; A. Gilles, "Un Témoignage inédit de l'enseignement de Philippe de Vitry," in *MD*, X (1956), 35.

22

ROBERT DE HANDLO. *Regulae cum maximis magistri Franconis, cum additionibus aliorum musicorum.* 1326.

This work presents the most exhaustive study, in a medieval treatise, of the notational means that were required to portray accurately the rhythmic complexities of the polyphonic music of the late 13th and early 14th centuries. Many of the participants in the conversation that forms the substance of the treatise are known to us from other theoretical writings, e.g., Johannes de Garlandia, Franco of Cologne, and Petrus de Cruce; others include Robert de Handlo himself, Petrus le Viser, and Admetus de Aureliana. The apparently excessive range of note values (from the duplex long to the minim) reflects the actual musical notation of the time, which tended in certain sources to use notes of greater value to express binary rhythm and in other sources to use notes of smaller value in keeping with the dissolution of the framework provided by the rhythmic modes. The extent to which Handlo supplies details enabling us to interpret the notation of his time may be illustrated by his treatment of the semibreve: he tells us that the smaller semibreve, representing the third part of a breve, is subject to ternary division and may be imperfected by a single minim *a parte ante,* and that the imperfect semibreve, called a *minorata semibrevis,* can also be imperfected *a parte post* in groups of notes set off by *signa rotunda* (hollow circles, such as are found in certain English sources). The main contribution of this treatise, however, is the exposition by Petrus le Viser of the three rhythmic *mores,* i.e., manners—long, medium, lively—of rendering the semibreve. (This information is important for our understanding of the rhythmic value of the semibreve in certain sources, e.g., Turin, *Biblioteca nazionale, Vari* 42.)

In Coussemaker, *Scriptores,* I, 383. See *M&L,* XXI (1940), 203 (comment by Manfred Bukofzer), and the review of Antoine Auda, "Les 'Motets Wallons' du manuscrit de Turin: Vari 42" by Luther Dittmer in *Die Musikforschung,* X (1957), 189.

23

JACQUES DE LIÈGE. *Speculum musicae.* (Formerly incorrectly attributed to Jean de Muris.) 1330-1340.

This voluminous and encyclopedic work consisting of seven books with 518 chapters is an impressive compilation of the important speculation and practical musical theory of the time. The various topics discussed include: the definitions and classification of music, as well as its inventors (Bk. I); intervals, consonances, and mathematical proportions (Bks. II-IV); music of the spheres (Bk. V); divisions of the monochord (Bks. V-VI); and polyphonic music of the 13th and 14th centuries (Bk. VII). Jacques had a definite predilection for the older music of the latter part of the 13th century and judged his contemporary composers by earlier standards; accordingly he opposed the tendency toward the imperfection of rhythmic values, since the older composers had written "so many beautiful and excellent songs, because they had never imperfected the duplex [long]." The identification of Franco of Cologne as a composer is perhaps as incorrect as the acceptance of "Aristotle" as the name of the author of the treatise by Lambertus (Coussemaker, *Scriptores,* I, 251 ff.), but Jacques's discourse on the division of the breve in the compositions of the learned composer Petrus de Cruce is much more authentic; wherever the breve is divided into more than three semibreves—as occurs in the motets attributed to Petrus, from which the author gives examples—the breve is apparently to have the same value as the long had previously had, causing a marked slowing down of the tempo of the parts written in long-breve notation.

Bks. VI and VII in Coussemaker, *Scriptores*, II, 193. Chs. 1-19 of Bk. I in Walter Grossmann, *Die einleitenden Kapitel des Speculum musicae* (1924). A complete ed. by Roger Bragard has been announced for publication in *CSM*. See also R. Bragard, "Le Speculum Musicae du compilateur Jacques de Liège," *MD*, VII (1953), 59; VIII (1954), 1. English trs. of portions of Bk. VII appear in Strunk, *Source Readings*, pp. 180 ff. See also Apel, *Notation*.

24

HUGO SPECHTSHART (VON REUTLINGEN). *Flores musicae omnis cantus gregoriani.* 1332; revised in 1338.

This work, interspersed with passages in verse, is an introduction to the musical theory of Gregorian chant. It reflects the need for a clarifying compilation of such theory late in the Middle Ages. The contents are centered mainly around four topics: solmization and the Guidonian hand, the monochord, intervals, and the modes. The last section includes a clear treatment of the formulas for the psalm tones, Magnificat, etc. The usefulness of the work as a pedagogical tool and its lasting influence are indicated by the fact that it was printed not only at Strasbourg in 1488, but at least once more at Leipzig in 1495.

With a German tr. by Carl Beck in the *Bibliothek des literarischen Vereins in Stuttgart,* LXXXIX (1868). See Robert Eitner, "Hugo von Reutlingen," *MfMG*, II (1870), 57; Paul Runge, *Die Lieder und Melodien der Geissler des Jahres 1347* (1900); and Hans J. Moser, *Geschichte der deutschen Musik,* I (1930).

25

ANONYMOUS. *Quatuor principalia.* (Formerly incorrectly attributed to Simon Tunstede.) Circa 1380.

Of the four divisions of this treatise, the first is concerned with definitions of music and speculations about it, the second with consonances and—in relation to them—proportions, and the third with the Guidonian hand and the ecclesiastical modes; the fourth discusses mensural music. In attempting to do justice to both sides with respect to the controversy still raging about the numbering of the rhythmic modes as well as with respect to the problem of the classification of the ligatures, the author presents the systems which a century before had been set forth by Franco of Cologne, on the one hand, and Lambertus (Pseudo-Aristotle), on the other (cf. Coussemaker, *Scriptores,* I, 117 and 251). Thus the Franconian doctrine, according to which the *proprietas* of a ligature in mensural notation is determined by the relationship the form of such a ligature bears to the corresponding original form in plainsong notation, is often confounded in the treatise with Lambertus' doctrine, according to which the *proprietas* is determined solely by the presence or absence of the stem. Of greater practical consequence for the understanding of music contemporary with this treatise are the discussions of (1) the rules of perfection and imperfection of smaller note values and (2) the various signs that indicate certain kinds of mensurations. Extensive space is given to a detailed presentation of the laws of voice leading. It is noted that the French and Italians seldom sing in parallel sixths above the plainsong.

In Coussemaker, *Scriptores,* IV, 200. An ed. by Gilbert Reaney has been announced for publication in *CSM.* The treatise of Anonymous I in Coussemaker, *Scriptores,* III, 334, varies only slightly from the fourth *Principale* (the section devoted to mensural music). See also Manfred Bukofzer, *Geschichte des englischen Diskants und des Faux-bourdons* . . . (1936); G. Reaney's remarks in *MD*, VIII (1954), 73; and Luther Dittmer, "The Ligatures of the Montpellier Manuscript," in *MD*, IX (1955), 45.

26

PROSDOCIMUS DE BELDEMANDIS. *Tractatus practice cantus mensurabilis ad modum Ytalicorum.* 1412.

The author believes the Italian system of notation to be superior to the French and deplores the declining use of the former. He therefore provides a clear exposition of the Italian system and points out its virtues by comparing it with the French system. The resulting work is one of our two most important sources of information concerning 14th-century Italian notation (the other being Marchettus de Padua's *Pomerium* of *c.* 1318). A thorough discussion of the divisions of *modus* and *tempus* includes some twenty rules governing the time-values of notes under various conditions. Prosdocimus states that the twofold nature of the *modus* and *tempus* mensurations (i.e., binary as well as ternary) is of Italian origin rather than French and, in this connection, that *ars Ytalica* is older than *ars Galica*. There are also brief sections on ligatures, rests, syncopation, diminution and augmentation, and musical repetition (to which Prosdocimus applies the terms *color* and *talea* interchangeably).

There are two versions of the work, both from the same year. The first is in Coussemaker, *Scriptores*, III, 228; but see also Claudio Sartori, *La notazione italiana del trecento* (1938), p. 26. The second, which, unlike the first, draws some material from Marchettus that conflicts with the Italian practice of Prosdocimus' time, is in Sartori, *ibid.*, p. 35. See Sartori also for further information concerning Prosdocimus and the two versions.

27

UGOLINO D'ORVIETO. *Declaratio musicae disciplinae.* Circa 1440.

Ugolino's treatise, based on Aristotle and Boethius as well as on late medieval philosophical and musical writings, deals with both the speculative and the practical aspects of music. The work consists of five books, with an appended treatise on the monochord; each book has an introduction treating of related philosophical matters. Book I discusses monophony; Book II, simple two-part polyphony. Book III is a study of Jean de Muris' *De musica mensurata.* Book IV deals with "the mathematical proportions and ratios of the material discussed in the first three books, defining those relationships which have been demonstrated in sound in terms of number." Book V is concerned with such speculative problems as the essence and the mathematical aspects of music. The appended study of the monochord contains highly valuable information on *musica ficta.*

An edition by Albert Seay is announced for early publication in *CSM,* VI. Excerpts in Adrien de la Fage, *Essais de diphthérographie musicale* (1864), pp. 116 ff.; A. W. Ambros, *Geschichte der Musik,* 5 vols. (3rd ed., 1887-1911), III, 147 ff.; and in the important article on which the above is largely based (and from which the quotation is taken): Albert Seay, "Ugolino of Orvieto, Theorist and Composer," in *MD,* IX (1955), 111. See also Utto Kornmüller, "Musiklehre des Ugolino von Orvieto," in *KJ,* X (1895), 19 (which translates or paraphrases a number of passages into German) and Gerhard Pietzsch, *Die Klassifikation der Musik von Boetius bis Ugolino von Orvieto* (1929).

THE RENAISSANCE

28

JOHANNES TINCTORIS. *Liber de arte contrapuncti.* 1477.

Tinctoris, who was in the employ of King Ferrante at
Naples, provides through the wide scope of his twelve
known treatises a key to the music theory of the whole Renaissance. The *Liber de arte contrapuncti* shows considerably
less of an unquestioning attitude toward authority than was
usual in most earlier writings: he says, in the prologue, that
music is not made by the spheres, as related by Boethius,
but only by instruments (including the voice). He is very
much a man of his time, for he asserts that, of older compositions, only those of the previous forty years are worth lis-
tening to. Contemporaries named by Tinctoris with admi-
ration at this point are Ockeghem, Regis, Busnois, Caron,
and Faugues, whose teachers, he says, had been Dunstable,
Binchois, and Dufay. The first of the three books that form
the body of the treatise provides a definition of counterpoint, to which an addition is made in Book II, showing
that to him the term is not only a generic one, embracing
both improvisation and written music, but also a specific
one, synonymous with "improvisation." The main subject
matter of Book I consists of the consonances. Tinctoris discusses twenty-two of them, from the unison to the tridia-
pason (the triple octave; i.e., he includes compound
intervals). The fourth, he says, is a consonance only in music in more than two parts and then only between upper
voices. Book II deals with the twenty-seven dissonances (including twelve "false consonances"—the diminished and
augmented fifth and octave and their compounds). Tinctoris quotes, with attributions, musical illustrations from

such composers as Faugues, Busnois, and Caron, thus making possible a correction of the wrong ascription of a Faugues Mass in Trent MS 88 to Ockeghem. He draws a distinction between dissonance treatment in written music and in improvisation: in the former, all the rules must be observed; in the latter, it suffices if the improvised lines are made to fit the tenor, though it is desirable that the singers have some understanding among themselves in advance. Book III includes his eight basic rules of counterpoint (see below).

In Coussemaker, *Scriptores* IV, 76, and *Johannis Tinctoris Tractatus de Musica* (1875), p. 198. English tr. of the prologue (dedication) in Strunk, *Source Readings,* pp. 197 ff. Many of the examples are given in modern notation in Ernest Ferand, *Die Improvisation in der Musik* (1939) and Ernst Krenek, *Hamline Studies in Musicology,* II (1947). See also Knud Jeppesen, *Counterpoint* (1939), and Reese, *Renaissance* (both of which include summaries of the eight basic rules of counterpoint).

29

JOHANNES TINCTORIS. *De inventione et usu musicae.* Circa 1485.

Although this work was originally written in five books, only a printed proof of some extracts survives. The copy opens with a letter to Johannes Stokhem, in which Tinctoris states that he has finished the treatise and is sending Stokhem two chapters each of Books II, III, and IV. This is what comes down to us. Chapters 19 and 20 of Book II are devoted to singing: the former deals with the singers of the Old Testament and of classical antiquity, the latter with the singers of the New Testament and of the author's own time. He discusses *cantus regalis,* a special kind of plainsong in which added notes ornament the *cantus planus.* Among the singers Tinctoris has known, he names Ockeghem as the finest bass. Chapter 8 of Book III deals with the history of the *tibiae* (wind instruments), their structure, and the material out of which they are made. Chapter 9 treats of the uses to which these instruments have been and are being put. In Tinctoris' own time they are widely employed at church festivals, weddings, banquets, processions, and similar public and private occasions. He states that in soldiers' camps and in the towns they are heard day and night. He praises Godefridus, who served Emperor Frederick III, as the best *tibia*-player of the time. Chapters 4 and 5 of Book IV are concerned with the *lyra* or *leutum* (lute) and its variants: the viol, rebec, guitar, citole, and *tambura*. Tinctoris credits the Catalans with having invented the guitar. In chapter 5 he writes about the best contemporary lutenists. In his opinion, the greatest of these is Pietro Bono at the court of Duke Hercules I of Ferrara. He states that the viol and rebec are *his* instruments, and he prefers to have them reserved for sacred music. The chapter ends with a discussion of the guitar and the *tambura*. Tinctoris says that the guitar is little used because of its thin tone and that women play it more than men. In Catalonia, however, men employ it in singing love songs. The *tambura* is an oriental lute-like instrument which was played in Italy by the Turkish invaders after they had been defeated at the battle of Otranto.

The six surviving chs. were published with commentary in 1917 by Karl Weinmann in *Johannes Tinctoris und sein unbekannter Traktat "De inventione et usu musicae"*; ch. 4 of Bk. IV also in Weinmann, "Ein unbekannter Traktat des Johannes Tinctoris," *Riemann-Festschrift* (1909), p. 267. Important extracts together with an English tr. thereof in Anthony Baines, "Fifteenth-century Instruments in Tinctoris's *De Inventione et Usu Musicae*," *The Galpin Society Journal*, III (1950), 19. See also Franz X. Haberl, "Ein unbekanntes Werk des Johannes Tinctoris," *KJ*, XIV (1899), 69; Reese, *Renaissance*.

30

GUILIELMUS MONACHUS. *De praeceptis artis musicae et practicae compendiosus libellus.* Circa 1480-1490.

This treatise opens with a discussion of time signatures, ligatures, and proportions. In an important subsequent section on English music, Guilielmus distinguishes two kinds of *fauxbourdon:* one in which the ornamented *cantus firmus* is in the treble and one in which the unornamented *cantus firmus* is in the tenor, i.e., at the bottom (this would be the type several historians, following the lead of Bukofzer, call "English discant"). Guilielmus provides details concerning the manner in which *fauxbourdon* should be written and also information regarding *gymel.* In addition he gives nine rules of counterpoint. In Rule 8, the syncope dissonance, or suspension, is mentioned for the first time in a known treatise on music.

A partial ed. in Coussemaker, *Scriptores,* III, 273; German tr. of a portion in Guido Adler, "Studie zur Geschichte der Harmonie," in *Sitzungsberichte der phil.-hist. Klasse der kais. Akademie der Wissenschaften in Wien,* XCVIII. Bd., III. Heft (1881), 790. See also Manfred Bukofzer, *Geschichte des englischen Diskants und des Fauxbourdons nach den theoretischen Quellen* (1936; errata list for the Coussemaker ed. on pp. 153 ff.) and "Fauxbourdon Revisited," *MQ,* XXXVIII (1952), 22; Heinrich Besseler, *Bourdon und Fauxbourdon* (1950); Curt Sachs, *Rhythm and Tempo* (1953); H. Hüschen in *MGG,* V, 1084 ff.

31

BARTOLOMÉ RAMOS DE PAREJA. *Musica practica.* 1482.

There are three parts to this work, Parts I and III being divided into sections (or treatises) and chapters, and Part II into chapters. The first section of Part I, after preliminary definitions, deals with the tuning of the monochord and solmization; the second, with melodic intervals and *musica ficta;* the third, with modes (tones), Greek nomenclature, and the interrelation of music with astrology. Part II is devoted to counterpoint. In Part III, section 1 covers various problems of mensural notation and the construction of canons; section 2 deals with proportionality and other miscellaneous problems. For his day, Ramos de Pareja was a revolutionary, and the *Musica practica* provoked heated controversy. Among the contested innovations was his method of tuning the monochord, by which, to obtain certain major and minor thirds of the 5:4 and 6:5 ratios, he sacrificed the purity of a fifth and a fourth. (This tuning approximated "just" intonation.) In the section on solmization he argued for a new system using eight syllables for the eight steps in the octave in place of the six steps of the Guidonian hexachord, a proposal that particularly offended the conservatives of his epoch.

Modern ed., with introduction by Johannes Wolf, in *BIMG,* 1. Folge, II (1901). English tr. of a portion in Strunk, *Source Readings,* pp. 201 ff.

32

FRANCHINO GAFORI. *Practica musicae.* 1496. (Later editions to 1512, with slight variations in title.)

The *Practica musicae,* the work of a leading writer in a particularly fruitful period for music theory, comprises four books, each containing fifteen chapters. Book I is devoted mainly to the church modes, while Book II is a thorough discussion of mensural notation. Book III, on counterpoint, contains Gafori's famous eight rules, most of which bear upon the use of the perfect consonances; *musica ficta* is also described. Book IV is one of the two most exhaustive Renaissance studies of proportions (the other being Tinctoris' *Proportionale musices* of *c.* 1475). Not only does Gafori treat such common proportions as the *sesquialtera* but, reflecting a period in which theorists had developed this aspect of the mensural system to a complexity that was quite unwarranted by the demands of practical music, he does not shrink from setting forth so unlikely a relationship as 4/19 (*proportio subquadruplasupertripartiensquartas*). The *Practica musicae* provides many valuable insights into the performance practice of the time. Thus Book I contains an account of differences between the Gregorian and Ambrosian chant formulas. A passage in Book III gives a very helpful indication of Renaissance musical tempo, for it equates the semibreve (the equivalent, at that time, of our modern quarter-note) to the "pulse beat of a quietly breathing man" —i.e., to M.M. 60 to 80. Also described is the strange practice, observed at the Milan Cathedral on occasions of mourning, of improvised polyphonic singing based on parallel seconds or fourths. Chapter 15 of Book III offers rules on performance and deportment for singers.

See E. Praetorius, *Die Mensuraltheorie des Franchinus Gafurius, BIMG,* 2. Folge, II (1905); Reese, *Renaissance;* C. Sartori in *MGG,* IV, 1237 ff.

33

SEBASTIAN VIRDUNG. *Musica getutscht.* 1511.

Written in the form of a dialogue, this is the earliest printed treatise on instruments. It is devoted mainly to describing the various types of instruments and to teaching the student how to transcribe vocal music for the organ, the lute, and the flute. Solmization, notation, tablature, the tuning of strings, and frets are also covered and the work concludes with a flute method. The text is embellished with a number of woodcuts showing many varieties of instruments, among which are the clavichord, virginal, lute, flute, bombard, zinck, trumpet, organ, drums, and many others.

Translations by Virdung's contemporaries include that into Latin by Luscinius (1536). Facs. eds., 1882, *PAPTM*, XI (Robert Eitner); and 1931 (with commentary by Leo Schrade). See Karl Nef, "Seb. Virdungs Musica getutscht," *Bericht über den Musikwissenschaftlichen Kongress in Basel (Neue Schweizerische Musikgesellschaft)* (1925).

34

ARNOLT SCHLICK. *Spiegel der Orgelmacher und Organisten.* 1511.

Schlick's treatise, the first work on organ construction printed in German, contains ten chapters and covers the materials to be used in the building of an organ, the erection and tuning of the instrument, its registration and contemporary use, descriptions of organs in existence in his day, and pitch, as well as various other technical matters.

Edited by Robert Eitner, in *MfMG*, I (1869), 77; ed. by Ernst Flade (1932; new ed. 1951). See also Raymond Kendall, "Notes on Arnold Schlick," *Acta*, XI (1939), 136.

35

GIOVANNI SPATARO. *Dilucide et probatissime demonstratione.* 1521.

In writing of the early 16th century, Jeppesen observes that a "music-theoretical madness, so to speak, . . . had seized all Italy. . . . One discussed music theory as today one discusses sport or the theatre." The publication of Ramos de Pareja's revolutionary *Musica practica* in 1482 set off a violent controversy among Italian and Spanish theorists which lasted for nearly half a century. Gafori, one of the writers who attacked the work of Ramos, is in turn attacked in the *Dilucide* by Spataro, Ramos' former pupil. The treatise is written in the form of a letter to Silvestro Alzato of Milan; its scurrilous treatment of Gafori is already indicated on the title page, which dubs him *Maestro de li errori*. The body of the work, however, is primarily a well-conceived attack on Gafori's opposition to the arithmetical method of measuring and classifying intervals and on his readiness to regard certain theoretical difficulties as "irrational" (insoluble). Spataro demonstrates that these difficulties must and can be solved; evading them simply leads to further problems. The discussion gives evidence of the difficulty encountered by theorists of the time who sought to reconcile contemporary practice and ancient theory.

Facsimile ed. by Johannes Wolf with a German introduction and tr. (1925). See also Knud Jeppesen, "Eine musiktheoretische Korrespondenz des früheren Cinquecento," in *Acta*, XIII (1941), 3, from which the above quotation is taken.

36

PIETRO ARON. *Thoscanello de la musica.* 1523. (Later editions, up to 1562, under the title *Toscanello in musica.*)

This general manual is the best-known work by Aron, a leading theorist of the first half of the 16th century. It includes discussion of mensural notation, intervals, and the three genera. A section on counterpoint, containing a set of rules that is unusually well formulated for the time, presents the first recommendation from a theorist that the parts of a polyphonic composition be conceived simultaneously. This establishes Aron's point of view as progressive, for he specifically states that many contemporary composers adhere to the older practice of writing the parts successively. An appendix that appears in later editions provides information on the polyphonic treatment of the modes and on the use of accidentals; in connection with the latter, Aron states that the composer ought to enter all the desired accidentals in the music and use uniform signatures rather than conflicting ones.

That the music theory of the time was caught in a struggle between contemporary practice and very old concepts is evident throughout the work. The intervals are defined in terms of both the Greek system and the medieval hexachord system, as well as by their numerical ratios. In the section on the intervals, these ratios are those of the Pythagorean measurements. Further on, however, in a section on the tuning of stringed keyboard instruments, Aron interestingly forsakes the Pythagorean system, recommending that fifths be shortened slightly so that pure major thirds may be obtained. Thus, despite the power of classical authority, Aron sets forth an early attempt at meantone temperament.

See Riemann, *Musiktheorie,* pp. 349 ff.; Edward Lowinsky, "The Concept of Physical and Musical Space in the Renaissance" in *Papers of the American Musicological Society for 1941* (1946); J. Murray Barbour, *Tuning and Temperament* (1951), pp. 26 f.; and Reese, *Renaissance.*

37

Martin Agricola. *Musica figuralis deudsch.* 1532.

This work is a continuation of the earlier *Ein kurtz deudsche Musica* (1528); also reissued in 1533 as *Musica choralis deudsch.* In contrast to Agricola's *Musica instrumentalis deudsch* (better known generally, since it was published in a modern edition by Eitner in 1896), this book is confined to vocal polyphony. It is copiously illustrated by examples taken from contemporary practice, which are accompanied by brief explanations. A thorough study of the elements of notation is given, followed by valuable and detailed discussions of time (including sections on *tactus,* augmentation and diminution, *punctus,* imperfection, alteration, etc.). The work concludes with an appendix of ten chapters devoted to proportions. This latter part shows the decided influence of Gafori.

See Heinz Funck, *Martin Agricola, ein frühprotestantischer Musiker* (1933).

38

SEBALD HEYDEN. *De arte canendi.* 1540. (Second edition of *Musicae, id est artis canendi libro duo,* 1537.)

Designed for the instruction of the boys at the St. Sebaldus school in Nuremberg, where Heyden was the rector, the *De arte canendi* is a clear and comprehensive musical manual, written in question-and-answer form. The author, a highly respected musician and teacher, writes for a practical purpose, and thus is less interested in restating outmoded principles out of respect for tradition than in providing dependable information regarding the musical practice of his time. Book I treats of such fundamentals as the gamut, solmization, and note-shapes; Book II deals with mensural notation and the modes. This work reflects the disintegration of the old church-mode system, induced by the demands of polyphony. In several respects, Modes VII and VIII are presented as having the character of major. For instance, in the musical example given to show the polyphonic application of Mode VII (twice transposed), the tenor, supplied with a signature of one flat (E never being flattened in the example), has F (rather than C) as the final. The *De arte canendi* contains many musical examples from contemporary and earlier composers; one of Ockeghem's two *catholica* (compositions intended to be performed in any one of several modes) is included, and the information Heyden gives about it provides modern scholarship with important clues leading to the correct resolution of the piece.

See Alfred Kosel, "Sebald Heyden," *Literarhistorisch-musikwissenschaftliche Abhandlungen,* VII (1940), 36 and *passim,* and Joseph S. Levitan, "Ockeghem's Clefless Compositions," in *MQ,* XXIII (1937), 440.

39

SILVESTRO DI GANASSI. *Regola Rubertina.* 1542-1543.

This two-volume work on music for the viols, named after the author's high-born pupil, Roberto Strozzi, is rich in valuable information. Ganassi considers viol playing from the aesthetic point of view, apparently for the first time in print, stating that *bellezza* (which means proper handling of the instrument, technique, etc.) and *bontà* (general musicianship and knowledge of music) are the two chief needs of the performer. In Part I, the first three chapters are devoted mainly to the proper manner of holding the viola da gamba and the best position of the body during performance. In chapter 4, Ganassi takes up the technique of the bow, saying that the index finger has the most to do with the control of dynamics. Chapters 5 and 6 are on left-hand technique. Chapters 7-10 give details on tuning the four members of the viol family (which each have six strings) for solo playing, while chapter 11 treats the same subject for ensemble playing. Here Ganassi refers to the use of the viol in works by Willaert, Jachet of Mantua, and Gombert. It is of some historic interest, in view of the oncoming *basso continuo* period, that he considers the bass viol the foundation for all the other parts. Chapters 12-14 are about viol tablature and the use of F, C, and G clefs. Chapters 15-17 deal with systems of tuning other than the normal one (i.e., with *scordatura*), to facilitate playing, and chapter 18 is about the custom prevalent among violists of playing their pieces a fourth higher than written, for the same reason. Illustrations are given. Chapters 19 and 20 present musical examples, including four *ricercari*, and chapter 21 is a summary of the volume. Part II is a much more advanced and detailed treatment of viol technique. The first of its three sections is devoted to the care and management of four-, five-, and six-stringed viols, and treats of such matters as tuning and choice and placement of strings. Other subjects are included, such as diminution (the breaking up of a long note into an aggregation of shorter ones), accompanying a vocal part, and playing *ricercari*, and there is information on the use of only four or three strings for solo playing. The second and third sections consist of polyphonic and solo *ricercari*, respectively.

Facsimile ed. by Max Schneider (1924). See Martin Greulich, *Beiträge zur Geschichte des Streichinstrumentenspiels im 16. Jahrhundert* (1934).

40

Heinrich Glareanus. *Dodecachordon*. 1547.

This landmark in the history of music theory is divided into three books of twenty-one, thirty-nine, and twenty-six chapters, respectively. Book I, based principally on Boethius and Gafori, deals with several aspects of traditional music theory: definitions of music, solmization, the structure of the gamut, mutation, transposition, consonance and dissonance, the smaller and larger semitones, the eight church modes, and music theory as applied to the monochord and some other stringed instruments; there is also a discussion of the section on the modes in Gafori's *De Harmonia instrumentorum musicorum opus*. This forms a prelude to

Book II which introduces the "new" modes, for which Glareanus is justly famous. Book II is concerned entirely with modal theory; to the eight traditional modes Glareanus proposes the addition of six, viz., the Aeolian, Hypoaeolian, Ionian, Hypoionian, Hyperaeolian, and Hyperphrygian modes. The first authentic plagal pair corresponds to natural minor, the second to major. The last two modes (now usually referred to as the Locrian and Hypolocrian) are dismissed by him as impractical, although, for purposes of illustration, he includes monophonic examples of all fourteen modes. Book III, which applies Glareanus' modal theories to the analysis of polyphonic music, begins with an exposition of mensural notation (including a chapter on the *tactus*) with examples based mostly on Gafori; it also contains numerous polyphonic examples by composers of the recent past, illustrating the twelve usable modes of Glareanus' system. The book concludes with mostly laudatory comments on the skill of Josquin des Prez, Pierre de la Rue, Ockeghem, Obrecht, Brumel, Isaac, and Mouton.

An English tr. in H. M. Miller, "Henricus Glareanus: Dodecachordon," unpublished (except in microfilm) Ph.D. dissertation, University of Michigan (1950). A German tr. by P. Bohn in *PAPTM,* XVI (1888). An English tr. of Bk. III, ch. 24, in Strunk, *Source Readings,* pp. 219 ff. See also Ernst Kirsch, "Studie zum Problem des Heinrich Loriti (Glarean)," *Festschrift A. Schering* (1937); H. Albrecht in *MGG,* V, 215 ff.

41

Juan Bermudo. *Declaración de instrumentos musicales.* 1555.

Although the title page states that this work includes six books, there are actually only five. The first and second largely duplicate Bermudo's previously published *Libro primero dela declaración de instrumentos* (1549). Book I contains praises of music collected from ancient writers; Book II teaches the rudiments of plainsong and mensural music, and introduces the student to the *monachordio* * (keyboard instrument), guitar, and vihuela of six courses; Book III delves much more deeply into plainsong, explaining what accidentals may be used, and then treats some of the more advanced problems of mensural theory. Book IV introduces the student to a wide variety of keyboard and stringed instruments, and tells him how to play with "great science and art." This book contains valuable charts of keyboard and plucked stringed instruments used in Spain, tells how to tune them, explains how modes affect instrumental music, shows a unique system of ciphering keyboard music on four horizontal lines (each of which represents a voice part), and explains the common method of ciphering vihuela music. In this book Bermudo describes several "new" types of vihuela, including one with seven instead of the customary six courses. At the end of Book IV, he inserts thirteen pages of his own original organ music, the parts being printed separately on five-line staves. Book V contains an introduction to the art of composition which, for Bermudo, includes the preparatory science of writing and improvising counterpoint above a given plainsong. Book VI, which was not printed, was to have contained animadversions against other Spanish theorists.

Bermudo was well read in foreign as well as Spanish theoretical works, and understood the roots of the more notorious controversies raging in his time. His acquaintance with contemporary music was also extensive, and much interest attaches to his asides on "modern" music. He was a progressivist and looked on earlier music as belonging to the "old dispensation."

Facsimile ed. by Macario Santiago Kastner, in Series I of *Documenta Musicologica* (1957). See Otto Kinkeldey, *Orgel und Klavier in der Musik des 16. Jahrhunderts* (1910).

* Bermudo's spelling.

42

NICOLA VICENTINO. *L'Antica musica ridotta alla moderna prattica*. 1555.

In *L'Antica musica,* Vicentino, a pupil of Willaert and apostle of "advanced" music, applies what he believes to be the ancient Greek diatonic, chromatic, and enharmonic genera to the polyphonic music of his time. His enharmonic system divides the whole tone into five parts. His chromaticism reflects the increased freedom of his time with regard to the diatonic restrictions of the modal system and the desire to express to a greater degree the emotions inherent in the words upon which a vocal composition is based. The work consists of a preface and five books. In Book I, Vicentino deals with intervals of various types (e.g., there are several types of semitones). Book II is concerned mainly with the connection of harmonic intervals. Book III deals at first with elementary composition and leads up to chromatic and enharmonic composition. In Book IV finer points in composing for various numbers of voices are discussed. In this book there is also an account of Vicentino's dispute with Lusitano. Book V is a method for the archicembalo, the instrument that Vicentino created for playing the various smaller intervals whose use he advocated.

See Hermann Zenck, "Nicola Vicentinos 'L'Antica musica,' " *Theodor Kroyer-Festschrift* (1933), p. 86.

43

HERMANN FINCK. *Practica musica*. 1556.

This work is best known for its information about vocal embellishment. In his introduction, Finck speaks of his distinguished uncle, Heinrich Finck, and numerous other composers. The treatise is in five parts: the first deals with notes, intervals, solmization, etc.; the second with mensural notation; the third with canons; the fourth with the modes (and includes valuable remarks on instrumental practices of Finck's time); while the fifth is devoted to the ornamentation of vocal music. Finck recommends that ornamentation be applied to all of the voices, but to only one voice at a time so that the embellishment may be heard clearly; moreover, ornamentation should not be used when there is more than one singer to a part. The work is profusely illustrated with musical examples, including a complete motet with its ornamentation written out.

A German tr. of Pt. V in *MfMG,* XI (1879), 129. See *PAPTM,* VIII (1879), xiii; A. W. Ambros, *Geschichte der Musik,* 5 vols. (3rd ed., 1887-1911), III, 229; Reese, *Renaissance;* H. Albrecht in *MGG,* IV, 205, 214 f.; Imogene Horsley, "Improvised Embellishment in the Performance of Renaissance Polyphonic Music," *JAMS,* IV (1951), 12.

44

GIOSEFFO ZARLINO. *Le Istitutioni harmoniche.* 1558 (later editions to 1589).

Pupil of Willaert and successor to Cipriano de Rore as *maestro di cappella* at St. Mark's in Venice, Zarlino was one of the celebrated musicians of his time. As a theorist he possessed erudition and great originality. Thus his writings are valuable both for the light they shed on the musical practice of the mid-16th century and as extremely influential contributions to the historical development of music theory.

The *Istitutioni,* Zarlino's chief work, is divided into four parts. The first contains some general material on the nature and value of music, but is mainly devoted to mathematical aspects of the art. Considerable stress is laid on the integers 1-6; taken in the order 1:2:3:4:5:6, any pair of consecutive numbers provides the ratio for a consonant interval, and as a consequence this *senario* (or set of six) plays an important role in Zarlino's harmonic theory. Part II discusses ancient theory, the consonances, the three genera, tuning systems, and the emotional effects produced by music. He recognizes the correctness of Ptolemy's syntonic diatonic (a tuning that is equivalent to modern "just" intonation); his view was later to be attacked by his former pupil Galilei (47), who preferred Pythagorean tuning. Part III, dealing primarily with principles of counterpoint, includes one of the earliest thorough discussions of double counterpoint. Chapter 10 contains a historically important statement concerning the major and minor triads (though Zarlino does not use these terms); he notes the difference between their auditory effects, and describes the major triad as arising from the harmonic division of the perfect fifth (which produces the relationship 4:5:6), and as therefore being in accordance with the order of the *senario*. The minor triad, he writes, results from the arithmetical division of the perfect fifth (6:5:4), and is therefore contrary to the order of the *senario*. Part IV contains a thorough discussion of the twelve church modes. The order in which they are presented in later editions (after the publication of Zarlino's *Dimostrationi harmoniche,* 1571) is of historical interest, for there the Ionian modal pair corresponding to modern major is shifted from last place to first in the series. Chapter 32 stresses the importance of expressing in the music the mood of the text. Chapter 33 includes Zarlino's famous ten rules for setting text to music.

English tr. of several extracts (including the ten rules) in Strunk, *Source Readings,* pp. 228 ff. See also Matthew Shirlaw, *The Theory of Harmony* (1917), pp. 29 ff. and *passim;* Fritz Högler, "Bemerkungen zu Zarlinos Theorie," in *ZfMW,* IX (1927), 518; Hermann Zenck, "Zarlinos 'Istitutioni harmoniche' als Quelle zur Musikanschauung der italienischen Renaissance," in *ZfMW,* XII (1930), 540; and Reese, *Renaissance.*

45

Tomás de Sancta Maria. *Libro llamado Arte de tañer Fantasia assí para Tecla como para Vihuela.* 1565.

In his detailed discussion of instrumental technique, particularly that of the keyboard, Sancta Maria gives us much information regarding performance practice in his day. The work is divided into two parts, the first being concerned with keyboard playing, the second with the technical subjects of which one required knowledge if one was to improvise, i.e., intervals, counterpoint, cadences, etc. He treats of such matters as hand position, fingering, ornaments, and the qualities of good performance. The book is of particular value since it provides one of our earliest sources dealing systematically with fingering. Thus, besides recommending that one play cleanly, in good time, and with taste, he provides different fingerings for different tempos. The practice of improvisation in instrumental style is analyzed, and the chapter on learning to "play fantasy" is of major importance.

Partial German trs. in Otto Kinkeldey, *Orgel und Klavier in der Musik des 16. Jahrhunderts* (1910) and Eta Harich-Schneider and Ricard Boadella, *Fray Tomás de Sancta Maria, Wie mit aller Volkommenheit und Meisterschaft das Klavichord zu spielen sei* (1937). See also Ernst Ferand, *Die Improvisation in der Musik* (1938).

46

Francisco Salinas. *De musica libri septem.* 1577.

This treatise contains lengthy and precise explanations of the mathematical ratios of sounds in various systems of tuning, and is richly accompanied by geometrical illustrations. Book I defines the proportions and proportionality.

Book II treats of the basic consonances (among which Salinas includes the fourth) and then turns to dissonant intervals. In Book III he examines the diatonic, chromatic, and enharmonic genera of the ancient Greeks with greater fidelity to classical sources than perhaps any other writer in his century. At chapter 13 of Book III he begins his explanation of temperament, which for keyboard instruments involves the proper distribution of the comma. Salinas is usually credited with having invented the 1/3-comma meantone temperament. Toward the close of Book IV he reviews the findings of such prominent 16th-century theorists as Glareanus, Fogliano, and Zarlino. Books V, VI, and VII deal with problems of meter and rhythm, and include copious illustrations from the Greek, Latin, and Spanish poets. Of great interest in these last books are the musical illustrations, which include a number of Spanish folk songs as well as some that Salinas heard at Rome and Naples. These range from street cries to such tunes as *Yo me iba, mi madre*, a tune found two hundred years earlier in the *Libre Vermell* of Montserrat; two songs illustrating the rhythm of the Portuguese folías; and the much-discussed *Rey don Alonso, Rey mi señor*, which Salinas thought to have been originally a Moorish tune.

Sir John Hawkins summarized this treatise in his *A General History of the Science and Practice of Music*, 5 vols. (1776), chs. 85-87. See also Riemann, *Musiktheorie*, pp. 394 ff., and J. B. Trend, "Salinas: A Sixteenth Century Collector of Folk Songs," *M&L*, VIII (1927), 13.

47

VINCENZO GALILEI. *Dialogo . . . della musica antica e della moderna.* 1581.

This treatise is written in the form of a dialogue between Giovanni Bardi, the leader of the *Camerata* (a Florentine group active in promoting monodic music shortly before

1600) and Piero Strozzi, another member of the organization. Galilei's main purpose is to further the cause of monodic music, but he also deals with tuning, modal theory, counterpoint, music history, and contemporary instrumental music. His discussion of tuning leads him into a controversy with his teacher, Zarlino (44), who had claimed that the vocal intonation of the period conformed with that of Ptolemy. Galilei held that the intonation was actually a compromise between the Pythagorean (with its pure fifths) and the Ptolemaic (with its consonant thirds). The *Dialogo* provoked a reply from Zarlino which was in turn answered by Galilei in 1589. The controversy was ended only with the death of Zarlino in 1590. When, in the *Dialogo*, Galilei draws a comparison between polyphony and monody, in which the latter is greatly favored, he is indebted to Girolamo Mei. Galilei believes that a text can best be expressed in music through monody, the method used by the ancient Greeks. He gives, in Greek notation, what he claims are old Greek hymns to the Muse, the Sun, and Nemesis (at least some of this music being attributed to Mesomedes of Crete, a shadowy figure who is conjectured to have flourished *c.* A.D. 130); in doing so he becomes our earliest source for these pieces. Although the tables of Alypios (which provide us with the key for deciphering Greek notation) survive complete elsewhere, it is of interest that, in this treatise, Galilei is the first to have made some of them available in print.

Facsimile ed., with preface by Fabio Fano, *Bollettino Bibliografico Musicale* (1934); partial ed., with commentary by Fabio Fano (1947). English tr. of a portion in Strunk, *Source Readings,* pp. 302 ff. See also C. Palisca in *MGG,* IV, 1265 ff.

48

Ludovico Zacconi. *Prattica di musica.* Part I, 1592; Part II, 1622.

Each of the two parts of the *Prattica* is divided into four books. In Part I, the first book has sections on the emotional effects of music, music as a science, music history, the elements of music, etc., as well as a comprehensive treatment of the art of the singer with copious musical examples, among them exercises, this treatment including such topics as vocal method, ornamentation, and enunciation. There are discussions on the responsibilities of the singer, of the director of music, and of the composer, and a brief section on the *villanella* and the *canzonetta*. Book II is devoted entirely to the problems of mood, time, and prolation. Book III takes up the proportions, including a chapter on the varying opinions of *alcuni particolari professori* on the subject. An especially interesting feature of this book is a *Tavola universale de' diversi essempii di proportione,* with musical quotations taken from the works of a large number of composers, going as far back as Ockeghem. Book IV has to do with the twelve modes and also contains brief sections on various instruments. In Part II, the first book covers some of the same material as does the corresponding section of Part I, but without a discussion of singing. Book II begins a discussion of the technique of counterpoint that includes (commencing with ch. 15) the five species of counterpoint that had been foreshadowed by Diruta (49) and were later—from Fux on—to become a standard pedagogical tool. There is a chapter on the importance of teaching *contrappunto alla mente* (i.e., improvisation), and the ensuing chapters take up various aspects of written counterpoint. Included, for instance, are several examples of how to set against each other the *Salve Regina,* the *Regina coeli,* the *Ave Regina,* and the *Alma Redemptoris Mater,* using each in turn as a *cantus firmus* and placing the others against it in freer form, first one at a time, then all three together. Book III takes up the more complicated aspects of contrapuntal technique, such as canon at various pitch and time intervals, direct and in contrary motion, without and with a *cantus firmus.* Imitation also receives careful attention. There are whole sections of musical examples (with discussion) taken from the works of Tigrini, Cerreti, Zarlino, Banchieri, and Diruta. Book IV continues the subject and concludes with a discussion of actual composition, with sections on writing for two, three, and four voices.

See Friedrich Chrysander, "Lodovico Zacconi als Lehrer des Kunstgesanges," *VfMV,* VII (1891), 337; IX (1893), 249 (which contains a German tr. of much of Pt. I, Bk. I); X (1894), 531.

49

Girolamo Diruta. *Il Transilvano.* Part I, 1593; Part II, 1609.

As far as is known, this *dialogo* is the first thoroughgoing method written for organists and cembalists. Diruta, a former pupil of Merulo, Porta, and Zarlino, writes with authority on the Venetian keyboard technique of his time. Particularly important is his distinction between the technique of the organ and that of the cembalo.

Part I deals with ornaments and such technical matters as hand position and fingering, and includes seventeen *toccate* by the author and several of his famous contemporaries. Some of these pieces are actually "studies" (i.e., pieces based on specific technical problems) and appear to be our earliest keyboard études. Part II begins with a discussion of the intabulation of vocal compositions and provides examples of five types of elaboration proper to a keyboard arrangement. The following section, on counterpoint, presents its material in a "species" arrangement, much like the one that was to be developed by Zacconi and transmitted to modern musicians by Fux. The section also includes twelve *ricercari* by Diruta and others. A discussion of the modes and transposition is followed by a set of keyboard settings (by some of the same composers) of hymns in the twelve modes.

See Carl Krebs, "Girolamo Diruta's Transilvano," in *VfMW*, VIII (1892), 307, which reproduces many passages from the treatise in German tr. For bibliographical and other information see also E. Haraszti in *MGG*, III, 556 ff.

50

HERCOLE BOTTRIGARI. *Il Desiderio overo de' Concerti di varij strumenti musicali.* 1594.

A treatise written in the form of a dialogue, the *Desiderio* is the author's most important work. It is mainly concerned with the practical problems of ensemble performance, including the tuning of instruments in order that they may be played together. Like Zarlino, Bottrigari classifies instruments in three categories according to the nature of their tuning: (1) those of a fixed pitch that cannot be changed readily by the performer, e.g., the organ, harpsichord, and harp; (2) those whose tuning is fixed by frets or fingerholes, which allow the performer to make only slight adjustments of pitch, e.g., the lute, viola da gamba, and flute; and (3) those whose pitch is completely alterable, e.g., the trombone, viola da braccio, and lyra da braccio. Bottrigari shows that the lute cannot play in tune with the harpsichord because the instruments are tuned in different systems. Although he does not actually expound a new system of intonation, his remarks foreshadow Artusi's modified meantone temperament. The treatise includes a discussion of the use of the voice with instruments as well as valuable accounts of various actual instrumental and vocal ensembles, active mainly at Ferrara.

Facsimile ed. by Kathi Meyer, P. Hirsch Library publication No. 5 (1924). See also G. R. Hayes, *Musical Instruments and their Music 1500-1750* (1928-30), Vol. II; D. P. Walker in *MGG*, II, 154 ff.; J. M. Barbour, *Tuning and Temperament* (1951); Reese, *Renaissance*.

51

ADRIANO BANCHIERI. *Conclusioni nel suono dell'organo.* 1609 (other editions from 1591 to 1627).

A composer of lively madrigal comedies and a leading Bolognese musician of the late Renaissance and early Baroque, Banchieri produced a number of musical writings that provide valuable information concerning instrumental practice during the rise of the concerted style and the *basso continuo.* The *Conclusioni,* despite its title, is really a set of twenty brief chapters on various musical subjects treated from the organist-choirmaster's standpoint. After a short review of the history of the organ, Banchieri gives an account of notable contemporary Italian organs, their players, and their builders. Further on, he traces the rise of the new musical style, praising the clear declamation in Viadana's *Cento concerti ecclesiastici* (1602). A discussion of specific uses of the organ throughout the church year stresses the performance of Masses, Magnificats, hymns, etc., in alternation style (in which singers and organ take turns in presenting successive portions of the music). In a section devoted to the various types of organ playing, he reports that the *basso seguente* is much in use. (This term normally applies to the kind of organ bass that duplicates the melodic line of the vocal bass, or of whatever part happens to be functioning as the lowest one at any given moment, and which an organist was expected to derive from the parts in question if he was accompanying in the performance of a polyphonic work.) Banchieri deplores the laziness of some organists who confine their activity to the playing of *bassi seguenti* to such an extent that they lose their skill in playing real organ music. But he concedes the value of these *bassi* and recommends that every organist seek to play them according to good rules. After briefly treating consonant and dissonant intervals, mensural notation, and the modes, he prescribes the method for tuning keyboard instruments. The first of the several appendices is particularly interesting, as it sets forth the tunings required of various stringed instruments for ensemble performance with organ or harpsichord; the instruments specifically named are the lute, in three different sizes; the viol, in four sizes; and the violin, in three sizes. In a discussion of modern music, Monteverdi is singled out for the highest praise. A copy of a letter devoted to keyboard fingering from Banchieri to an organ virtuoso is included. Another letter, from Agostino Agazzari to an unnamed Sienese virtuoso, deals with the role of voices and instruments in concerted music.

Facsimile ed., *Bollettino Bibliografico Musicale* (1934).

52

COSTANZO ANTEGNATI. *L'Arte organica*. 1608.

Antegnati came from a long line of North Italian organ builders; altogether there were eight generations. *L'Arte organica* was written for Antegnati's youngest son, who became his helper. In it he lists the 145 organs he had built up to the time of writing. It contains, in the form of a dialogue with his son, the history of the family, the requirements of a church organ, methods of voicing, registration, and descriptions of several Antegnati organs. The most important feature of *L'Arte organica* is the description of twelve different methods of registration that may be employed by organists in the performance of preludes and introits in church. Antegnati discusses also the function of the organist in providing suitable responses to the chanting of the celebrant in the observance of the Mass.

In an ed. by Renato Lunelli, with a German tr. by Paul Smets (1938). See also P. Guerrini, "La Bottega Organaria degli Antegnati," *Bollettino del Consiglio e Ufficio Provinciale dell'Economia* (1930).

53

DOMENICO PIETRO CERONE. *El melopeo y maestro.* 1613.

This huge synthesis, divided into twenty-two books and extending to 1160 pages, begins its discussion of plainsong in Book III, arrives at mensural theory in Book VI, discusses the art of vocal and instrumental variation in Book VIII, and teaches the art of counterpoint in Books IX and X. Book XIV treats of canon and fugue in the early 17th-century sense of those terms. The later books deal with the higher problems of composition, of mensural theory, and of "tonality" in polyphonic music. In Book XX Palestrina's *Missa L'Homme armé* (1570) is minutely analyzed—this being, for Cerone, the most "learned" of Palestrina's masses. The last book deals with musical enigmas and puzzle canons. Cerone scatters through his twenty-two books a vast number of references to leading musicians of the 16th and early 17th centuries.

A few chs. with commentary in F. Pedrell, *Los músicos españoles antiguos y modernos en sus libros* (1888), I, 40. English tr. of a portion of Book XII in Strunk, *Source Readings,* pp. 263 ff. See also Ruth Hannas, "Cerone's Approach to the Teaching of Counterpoint," *Papers of the American Musicological Society* (1937), p. 75, and "Cerone, Philosopher and Teacher," *MQ,* XXI (1935), 408; H. Anglès in *MGG,* II, 969 ff.

FROM THE BAROQUE TO THE
20TH CENTURY

54

MICHAEL PRAETORIUS. *Syntagma musicum.* Volume II, 1618; another edition, 1619; Appendix (*Theatrum instrumentorum*) for Volume II, 1620; and Volume III, 1619.

Volume I (Latin, 1615) is the least important from the standpoint of original contribution. It is concerned with the music and instruments of the ancients and the ecclesiastical music of the Roman Church. Volumes II and III (both in German) emphasize the practical and contemporaneous rather than the theoretical and historical. Volume II contains a detailed treatment of the musical instruments in use at the time, the greatest stress being laid on the evolution and construction of the organ. This volume is divided into five parts. Part I treats of the nomenclature and classification of musical instruments. Part II contains descriptions of the form, compass, quality of tone, etc., of these instruments. Part III treats of ancient organs, giving valuable information concerning their form and construction. Modern organs are described in Part IV. Part V is devoted to certain individual organs, celebrated for the excellence of their tone or for their size. At the end there is an appendix of several sets of organ specifications. This is followed by a "Theater of Instruments," which contains forty-two woodcuts of instruments. Volume III is in three parts. The first covers many of the forms of composition practiced in Praetorius' day (concerto, motet, *falsobordone,* madrigal, *canzona, ricercar, sinfonia,* sonata, dance forms, etc.). Part II deals with theory, notation, rhythm, and choruses, and has some information on performance practice. Part III has explanations of musical terms (*ritornello, ripieno,* etc.) and tells how organists and others should realize figured basses. It shows how instruments can be combined, that is, how various types of ensembles may be used. There is also a section on choral music and ornamentation.

Facsimile of Vol. II ed. by Wilibald Gurlitt (1929); diplomatic reprint of Vol. II ed. by Robert Eitner in *PAPTM,* XIII (1884). English tr. of Pts. I and II of Vol. II by Harold Blumenfeld, *De organographia* (1949). Modern ed. of Vol. III (*Kritisch revidierter Neudruck nach dem Original*) by Eduard Bernoulli (1916).

55

JOHANNES CRÜGER. *Synopsis musica.* 1630 (enlarged 1654).

One of the earliest complete instruction books on composition written in the 17th century, this book is clearly representative of the transitional character of its time, as may be seen in its simultaneously conservative and progressive nature. A forward-looking aspect may be noted in Crüger's emphasis on the triad (which, incidentally, stands for perfection, since it symbolizes the Holy Trinity) with its resultant harmonic implications. Such aspects appear also in the importance given to thorough-bass and the doctrine of "affects." With regard to the latter point, it is of some interest that Crüger advocates transposing the modes to accord with whatever "affect" the composer wishes to depict. He recommends using the bass rather than a *cantus firmus* as the point of departure for a composition. Among the other subjects covered are solmization and four-part writing. The work on the whole is of value less for its originality than as a clear compendium of the theories of its time. To a large extent it is based on earlier writers, such as Zarlino, Lippius, Calvisius, M. Praetorius, and Herbst.

See E. Fischer-Krückeberg, "Johannes Crüger als Musik-theoretiker," *ZfMW*, XII (1929), 609; W. Blankenburg in *MGG*, II, 1799 ff.; Ralph Harold Robbins, *Beiträge zur Geschichte des Kontrapunkts von Zarlino bis Schütz* (1938).

56

MARIN MERSENNE. *Harmonie universelle*. 1636.

Its encyclopedic length, scientific approach, and the comprehensiveness and variety of its subject material, all help to make the *Harmonie universelle*—which was held in high esteem by Mersenne's contemporaries—a veritable treasure house of information about early Baroque music and its practice. The work is divided into five treatises. The first is on the nature of sounds and movements. It includes studies of the physics of sound and its production, the properties of "harmonic" strings and other bodies. The second treatise is on the mechanics of weights. The third is on the voice and singing, including an analysis of the voice and the anatomical mechanism that produces it. There is a table of 720 possible combinations of the scale degrees ut, re, mi, fa, sol, la. Discussions of dance pieces and meter are also presented. The next treatise is on consonance and dissonance. It deals with genera, species, systems, modes, etc., concluding with the art of composition. The last treatise is on instruments. After a classification of instruments, there is a book on the lute, its tuning, the way to play it, and its tablature. Following this there are books on the spinet, the violin, wind instruments, the organ, percussion instruments, the use of harmony, and "other mathematical points." Many large and clear illustrations of instruments are provided.

See Hellmut Ludwig, *Marin Mersenne und seine Musik-lehre* (1935).

57

CHRISTOPH BERNHARD. *Von der Singe-Kunst oder Manier* and *Tractatus compositionis augmentatus* (both in MS). Circa 1657.

Von der Singe-Kunst is concerned with ornamentation as it was used in vocal music. The *Tractatus compositionis augmentatus* represents an ambitious attempt to bring old and new musical theories into a clear, unified system. The work may be considered an expression of the musical theories of Heinrich Schütz, whose pupil Bernhard was. It deals extensively with counterpoint. Two styles are discussed: *stylus gravis (stylus antiquus)* and *stylus luxurians (stylus modernus)*. The *stylus gravis* places greater emphasis on the music than on the text. Bernhard divides the *stylus luxurians* into two substyles: *communis* and *comicus* (or *theatralis* or *oratorius* or *recitativus*). Within the first of these, *communis,* music and text are of equal importance. Within the second, *comicus,* the text absolutely dominates the music. This is the pure theatrical substyle. Bernhard discusses rhetorical figures that may be employed in the *stylus luxurians comicus.* Among them are *ellipsis, mora, abruptio, tertia deficiens,* and *sexta superflua.* He does not identify his main styles with types of composition, such as church, chamber, or theatrical music, but rather with the manner in which melody and dissonance are treated and with the relationships between text and music.

Both works in J. M. Müller-Blattau (ed.), *Die Kompositionslehre Heinrich Schützens in der Fassung seines Schülers Christoph Bernhard* (1926). See also Ralph Harold Robbins, *Beiträge zur Geschichte des Kontrapunkts von Zarlino bis Schütz* (1938).

58

WOLFGANG CASPAR PRINTZ. *Historische Beschreibung der edelen Sing- und Kling-Kunst.* 1690.

This is not only the first chronicle of music, but also a work especially important for an account of 17th-century musicians. In the preface Printz says that much of his material was destroyed by fire, so that the *Historische Beschreibung* is merely a collection of what remains. There are some borrowings from Praetorius in the work, these being German translations of selections from Volume I (Latin) of the *Syntagma.* The arrangement is as follows: chapters 1-7 are on music up to the time of Christ (ancient music and Greek and Hebrew instruments); chapter 8, on music up to the time of Gregory; chapter 9, on music from Gregory to the 10th century; chapter 10, on the 11th-15th centuries; chapters 11 and 12, on the 16th and 17th centuries respectively; chapter 13, on contemporary German church musicians; chapters 14-16, on various aspects of music; and chapter 17 is Printz's autobiography up to the age of forty-eight.

See Eugen Schmitz, "Studien über W. C. Printz als Musikschriftsteller," *MfMG,* XXXVI (1904), 100.

59

ANDREAS WERCKMEISTER. *Musikalische Temperatur.* 1691.

Werckmeister is famous for several theoretical works, among which are his *Orgelprobe.* His theories received a thorough survey in Mattheson's *Das forschende Orchestre* (1721). J. S. Bach undoubtedly knew Werckmeister's theories on temperament. In the *Musikalische Temperatur* Werckmeister deals with the tuning of keyboard instruments and the problem of the equal temperament of all twelve fifths of the circle. He says that only four of these twelve fifths should have the Pythagorean comma (c—g, g—d, d—a, b—f-sharp). To this effect he asserts in chapter 24 that "out of the circle of fifths it can be shown that not all the fifths may have the ¼ comma, or the circle will not be completed." Werckmeister's ideas are also expounded in his *Musicae mathematicae Hodegus curiosus, oder richtiger musikalischer Wegweiser* (1687), which is broader in scope.

See Walter Serauky, "Andreas Werckmeister als Musiktheoretiker," *Festschrift Max Schneider* (1935), p. 118.

60

JOHANN CHRISTOPH WAGENSEIL. *De Sacri Rom. Imperii Libera Civitate Noribergensi commentatio. Accedit, de Germaniae phonascorum Von der Meister-Singer . . . Sermone vernaculo liber.* 1697.

Part I, written in a rambling style, is in Latin with passages in Greek, Hebrew, and German. It is mainly a description of the city of Nuremberg. Part II (*Buch von der Meister-Singer holdseligen Kunst . . .*) is in German with passages in Latin, Greek, and Hebrew. Preceding it is a preface on the origin of gypsies. Chapter 1 is mainly an account of a long conversation between the author and a French authoress. In chapters 2 and 3 Wagenseil discusses the *Spruchsprecher,* who were extemporizers at social functions, and points out their inferiority to the Meistersinger. He tries to trace the origin of the Meistersinger to the Teutonic bards. The names of twelve men, whom he regards as the immediate ancestors of the Meistersinger, are included in chapter 4. Among these are Heinrich Frauenlob, Nicolaus Klingsohr, and Walther von der Vogelweide. Wagenseil also tells of a contest between Klingsohr and Wolfram von Eschenbach in which the black art of the former was vanquished by the piety of the latter. Chapter 5 is valuable as a complete *Tabulatur* of the Nuremberg Meistersinger, i.e., a set of the rules by which they composed. Chapter 6 is on the manners and customs of the Meistersinger and includes an account of their song-schools. The last chapter is devoted to a discussion of the usefulness of their art in daily life.

See C. Mey, *Der Meistergesang in Geschichte und Kunst* (1901); J. D. C. van Dokkum, "Der Meistersinger Holdse-lige Kunst," *Caecilia* (Amsterdam), LXV (1908), 465, 520.

61

LE CERF DE LA VIÉVILLE, SEIGNEUR DE FRENEUSE. *Comparaison de la musique italienne et de la musique françoise.* Part I, 1704; Part I, in a new edition, and Part II, 1705; Part III, 1706. All three parts reprinted in 1725 (and again in 1743) in the second edition of the *Histoire de la Musique* of Bourdelot and Bonnet.

The *Comparaison* has been called *"le premier essai véritable de critique musicale, developpée et raisonnée"* (from the French edition of the Riemann *Musiklexikon*). It is, at any rate, an early such attempt. Written by an ardent admirer of Lully and the French opera (i.e., the "classic" style), it replies to the *Parallèle des Italiens et des François* (1702) of the Abbé Raguenet, which supports Italian opera (i.e., the "modern" style). These two works, with Raguenet's response and a subsequent reply from Freneuse, are the opening guns in the battle between the proponents of French and Italian opera that raged through the greater part of the 18th century. The *Comparaison* is cast in the form of a dialogue for three people who discuss many aspects of operatic style. The fifth dialogue is devoted largely to Lully, and there is frequent mention of his works elsewhere. The sixth dialogue is a *Traité du bon goût en musique.*

English tr. of the sixth dialogue in Strunk, *Source Read-*

ings, pp. 489 ff. English tr. of Raguenet, *Parallèle*, also in Strunk, pp. 473 ff. and in *MQ*, XXXII (1946), 411. See Henry Prunières, "Le Cerf de la Viéville et l'esthétique musicale classique au XVII° siècle," in *S.I.M. (Revue musicale mensuelle)*, IV (1908), 619.

62

JEAN PHILIPPE RAMEAU. *Traité de l'harmonie réduite à ses principes naturels.* 1722.

A profoundly original thinker as well as the most important French composer of the 18th century, Rameau formulated many of the concepts that have remained at the core of Western harmonic theory to the present day. Although some of Rameau's ideas appear in mature form only in his later writings, the epoch-making *Traité*, his first theoretical work, contains the most essential of his principles. The work comprises four books. Book I and most of Book II are devoted to the generation and properties of the various intervals and chords. Here Rameau gives his account of the origin of harmonies in acoustical principles. From this he is able to develop a more systematic description of the invertibility of intervals than the one Zarlino (44) had offered in his *Dimostrationi harmoniche* (first ed. 1571). Rameau also applies the principle of invertibility to chords, and is thus the first to explain the essential identity that, for example, a C-major triad retains no matter which of its tones is in the bass at a given moment. Closely linked with this explanation is the idea, earlier expressed very briefly in Thomas Campion's *A New Way of Making Fowre Parts in Counter-Point* (1617?), but systematically explained by Rameau, that an interval has a fundamental note (or, in the modern term, a "root"); for example, that both the major third C-E and its inversion E-C have C as the fundamental note. Applying this idea to chords, he arrives at the concept of the fundamental bass (the succession of chord roots, as distinct from the actual bass part), which is regarded as the governing force in all chord successions. In Book III he applies his conception of harmony to the craft of the composer; in Book IV, to that of the keyboard accompanist. With respect to certain harmonic phenomena (e.g., the minor triad and the seventh chord) Rameau provides only unsatisfactory explanations, for he does not hesitate to struggle with problems that have troubled theorists even in our own time. Produced by one of the first-rate minds of the Age of Reason, the *Traité* is the real cornerstone in the modern theory of harmony.

English tr. of Bk. III, *A Treatise of Music, Containing the Principles of Composition* (1737?; republished 1752). English tr. of Bk. IV by Griffith Jones, *A Treatise on Harmony in which the Principles of Accompaniment are Fully Explained and Illustrated by a Variety of Examples* (1804?). English tr. of extracts from the preface and Bk. II in Strunk, *Source Readings*, pp. 564 ff. See also Matthew Shirlaw, *The Theory of Harmony* (1917?), pp. 63 ff. and *passim*.

63

JOHANN DAVID HEINICHEN. *Der General-Bass in der Composition.* 1728.

This treatise on figured bass is heavily indebted to Gasparini's *L'armonico practico al cembalo.* It is in two parts. In a lengthy introduction, Heinichen illustrates the *Affektenlehre* or doctrine of the "affects" by musical settings of Italian poems. Part I begins with a chapter on intervals and proceeds to one on chords; its remaining four chapters are devoted to the realization of figured basses, the use of florid passages in various time-signatures, examples in more difficult keys, and further refinements of figured-bass playing. Part II, also in six chapters, deals with the resolution of dissonance in music for the stage, the realization of unfigured basses, the accompaniment of recitatives, the application of the preceding rules to a complete cantata, the circle of keys and its practical use, and additional exercises. Heinichen's treatise greatly influenced later German writers, particularly Mattheson and J. G. Walther.

See F. Arnold, *The Art of Accompaniment from a Thorough-Bass* (1931), pp. 255 ff.

64

JOHANN MATTHESON. *Grosse General-Bass-Schule.* 1731.

Although this treatise is essentially a second edition of Mattheson's *Exemplarische Organisten-Probe* (1719), the entire contents have been thoroughly rewritten and greatly expanded. The treatise is one of the standard sources of information for music of the period, especially at Hamburg. It is devoted entirely to an exposition of thorough-bass practice. The work is divided into three parts: (1) basic preparatory material, (2) twenty-four easy examples, and (3) twenty-four examples of greater difficulty. Part I consists of 291 small sections, each dealing with some aspect of thorough-bass. A brief summary of the contents of each section is given in a list appended to this part. The forty-eight basses or "test pieces" in Parts I and II are intended as foundations for independent improvisations. In the explanatory notes that follow each "test piece" Mattheson particularly stresses imitative treatment in the upper parts of a phrase or figure that has occurred, or is about to occur, in the bass.

The English tr. of this work mentioned in Eitner's *Quellen-Lexikon*, VI, 385, is actually a partial tr. of Mattheson's *Kleine General-Bass-Schule*. See Beekman C. Cannon, *Johann Mattheson, Spectator in Music* (1947).

65

JOHANN MATTHESON. *Der vollkommene Capellmeister*. 1739.

Of encyclopedic proportions, this work by Mattheson synthesizes and systematizes his musical theories. It sets forth the precepts and knowledge necessary to an 18th-century director of a musical organization. It is divided into an introduction and three parts. In the introduction, Mattheson stresses the importance of good music in the church service and his belief that melody is the fundamental element of all music. Part I is a miscellany of information on various aspects of music. It has remarks on a "universal musical foundation" (by which is meant a song-like style of writing), on sound itself, musical literature and history, music in the state, pantomime, the mathematics of intervals, the art of writing melodies, modes and keys, and differentiation of style in composition for the theater and in instrumental, ecclesiastical, chamber, and canonic music. Part II is devoted entirely to the method and principles of writing a good "melody" (which seems to mean music generally). This part incorporates the complete text of Mattheson's *Kern melodischer Wissenschaft* (1737). In opposition to Rameau, Mattheson here confirms his belief that it is impossible for melody to spring from harmony; melody for him is "natural," harmony "artificial." This section covers melodies for dance pieces, oratorios, motets, and arias; the singing and playing of melodies; their rhythm and meter; ornamentation; and the expression of words. Part III deals with harmony and the rules of counterpoint and double fugue. At the conclusion there are three chapters on various practical matters, such as the construction of instruments (especially organs) and the art of performance.

Facsimile ed. by Margarete Reimann in Series I of *Documenta musicologica* (1954).

66

JOHANN GOTTFRIED WALTHER. *Musicalisches Lexicon oder Musicalische Bibliothec.* 1732.

Although this work is not actually the first dictionary of music, it might be thought of as such, since its comprehensive scope was unprecedented. According to the author, it owes its existence to the pleasure he took in supplementing Brossard's mere listing of some nine hundred names with more complete information about these people and their works. As a result of this "hobby" of the author's a valuable original source for biographical information about his contemporaries was created. Thus there are articles on Bach, Caldara, Graupner, Kuhnau, and Mattheson, to mention only a few of the more familiar figures. Walther, however, not only provides biographical articles, but lists and defines musical terms "used in Greek, Latin, Italian, and French." These, combined with twenty-two plates containing musical examples, constitute a prime source of information concerning Baroque performance practice, with regard to ornamentation, figured bass, and the doctrine of rhetorical figures in music, as well as concerning standard musical forms. As might be expected, considering the lack of precedents and the experimental methods Walther had to employ to collect information (he sent out letters of inquiry which were not always answered), there are some strange gaps; for example, there is no article on Handel. These gaps, however, hardly detract from the value of the work either as an intellectual achievement or as a source of information. Among the many authorities cited in this work Mattheson occurs most frequently.

Facsimile ed. by Richard Schaal, in Series I of *Documenta musicologica* (1953). See also Otto Brodde, *Johann Gott-*

fried Walther (1937), and Stanley Godman, "English Musicians in Walther's *Musicalisches Lexicon," Monthly Musical Record,* May, 1951, p. 97 (continued in subsequent numbers).

67

JOHANN ADOLPH SCHEIBE. *Der critische Musicus.* A weekly publication running from 1737 to 1740; collected and augmented edition, 1745.

This is the publication through which Scheibe is famous in the history of German opera. Among the vast range of topics discussed are the following: ancient music; the defects of German operas; the art of composition; descriptions of motets, sacred oratorios, theatrical music; an inquiry into chamber styles; the nature of cantatas without instruments; the nature of cantatas with one instrument; the qualities of a good organist; the art of writing fugues; the origin and nature of "symphonies"; a description of concertos; and a history of the decline of the Hamburg opera. Scheibe's greatest fame has derived from his attack (in his sixth number) on Bach. In the articles appended in the 1745 edition he published the "Impartial Comments on a Questionable Passage in the Sixth Part of *Der critische Musicus,"* written by Birnbaum in reply to Scheibe's derogatory remarks about Bach. Following this there is a "Reply to the Impartial Comments . . ." by Scheibe, which is in turn followed by Birnbaum's "Defence of his Impartial Comments. . . ." Also included in the 1745 edition are essays on the origin, growth, and nature of the current tastes in music; on musical styles; and on recitatives.

See Eugen Reichel, "Gottsched und Johann Adolph Scheibe," *SIMG,* II (1901), 654; Hans T. David and Arthur Mendel, *The Bach Reader* (1945), pp. 237 ff.

68

JOHANN JOACHIM QUANTZ. *Versuch einer Anweisung die Flöte traversiere zu spielen.* 1752.

Though ostensibly a flute method, this manual goes far beyond the limitations implied by its title. The way in which Quantz covers multitudinous details of 18th-century performance practice and taste is of inestimable value to modern students and performers. Some of the topics included are the history of the flute; its fingering, embouchure, phrasing, and tonguing; ornamentation; the playing of allegro and adagio (in the French and Italian manners); cadenzas; public performance; the art of accompaniment; the role of the concert-master; the playing of bowed string instruments and the clavier; orchestral performers; and musical criticism. The work is of special significance on the subject of tempo (it contains a table in which many tempos are related to the pulse beat), grace notes, the constitution of ensembles, dance movements, accent, intensity, etc. A series of informative examples is appended to the work.

Facsimile of the 3rd German ed. (1789), ed. by Hans Peter Schmitz, in series I of *Documenta musicologica* (1953). Critically revised reprint, with an introduction by Arnold Schering (1906). Trs. in French (1752) and Dutch (1754). English tr. (with minor omissions) of chs. 13-15 appeared under the title *Easy and Fundamental Instructions* with tables 13-21 of the original (c. 1790). Extract in English tr. in Strunk, *Source Readings,* pp. 577 ff. See also Arnold Dolmetsch, *The Interpretation of the Music of the XVII and XVIII centuries* (1916; 2nd ed., 1946).

69

GIUSEPPE TARTINI. *Trattato di musica secondo la vera scienza dell'armonia.* 1754.

In addition to being a virtuoso and pedagogue of high rank, Tartini was a theorist of considerable consequence. The *Trattato di musica,* the first of his musical treatises to be printed, consists of six sections, dealing with harmonic phenomena, the harmonic circle (i.e., the circle of fifths), musical systems, the diatonic scale, old and modern tonalities, and the intervals and modulations of modern music. The treatise is significant as the source of one of the first scientific explanations of what Tartini calls the "third" tone. (Although others anticipated him in print by a few years, the discovery may have been his, since he asserted that he had made use of the "third" tone as early as 1717 in teaching pure intonation to his violin pupils.) This "terzo suono" is the difference in tone that is heard below two notes in "just" intonation if they are sounded together loudly and clearly. Tartini recognizes a natural opposition between major and minor, and his *Trattato di musica* (preceded, however, by Rameau's *Génération harmonique,* 1737, and *Démonstration du principe de l'harmonie,* 1750) occupies a prominent position in the history of the theory —at one time widely credited—that minor harmony derives from an "undertone" series as major harmony is by many believed to derive from the overtone series. Owing to certain scientific deficiencies, Tartini's work was attacked by J. A. Serre, by Mercadier de Belesta, and later by J. J. Rousseau. Besides its importance as an exposition of theoretical opinion during the middle of the 18th century, it is valuable because of the material it contains on Dalmatian folk music of the period.

Several reference books mention a French tr. by P. Denis (*Traité des agréments de la musique,* 1782); this, however, is a tr. of another work, the original version of which has been lost. The *Trattato di musica* is discussed at length, with some disagreement, in J. A. Serre, *Observations sur les principes de l'harmonie*, pp. 109 ff., to which Tartini later replied. See also Matthew Shirlaw, *The Theory of Harmony* (1917?), pp. 287 ff.

70

Jacob Adlung. *Anleitung zu der musikalischen Gelahrtheit.* 1758; second edition, revised by J. A. Hiller, 1783.

While it would be more accurate to classify the *Anleitung* as a critical bibliography than in any other way, this would not do the author full justice. True, it was his main purpose to list all the works on musical subjects necessary to "educated music lovers and particularly to lovers of keyboard music, as well as to builders of organs and other instruments." Nevertheless, the author goes considerably beyond the requirements of his goal, since, besides listing available treatises (i.e., all those ever written, to his knowledge), he gives what might be called summaries of the problems treated in these works. Each of the twelve chapters of Part I and the eight chapters of Part II begins with a critical inventory of the literature relevant to the subject under scrutiny. This is followed by discussions of varying lengths for each chapter. The learning and objectivity that Adlung brings to his task make his treatise a valuable source of information about the opinions and controversies of his time on such subjects as appropriate church music, tuning, and solmization. Part I, which he calls "theoretical," has chapters on music in general, the history of music, acoustics, organs and organ registration, other keyboard instruments, and instruments "without keyboard." Part II— the practical part—has chapters on singing, thorough-bass, the chorale, tablatures, composition and improvisation, the teaching of keyboard playing, and the examination of candidates for musical positions. Despite its date of publication, the book is of great importance as a source of knowledge about Baroque performance practice, since Adlung was among those conservative musicians who, on occasion, have been charged with being behind their times. In addition, the work contains a good deal of source material of a biographical nature. Thus we find first-hand information about Pachelbel, the Bach family, and others. The book is preceded by an interesting preface written by one of Bach's distant relatives, Johann Ernst Bach, *Capellmeister* at the court of Sachsen-Weimar.

Facsimile ed. by Hans Joachim Moser in Series I of *Documenta musicologica* (1953).

71

FRANÇOIS BÉDOS DE CELLES. *L'Art du facteur d'orgues*. Part I, 1766; Parts II and III, 1770; Part IV, 1778.

The four parts of *L'Art*, richly illustrated with carefully executed plates, treat of the structure of the organ, methods of organ-building, advice to the organist, and descriptions of various instruments.

In Part I, chapter 1 contains a short discussion of various mechanical devices, such as levers and pulleys, that enter into organ building. Chapters 2 and 3 take up basic technical matters, including the tools of the organ builder, and there are suggestions on how to make things that cannot be purchased ready made. Chapters 4 and 5 deal with the constitution of various ranks of organ pipes, enumerating many of them and giving ranges and dimensions. Chapter 6 describes each separate part that enters into the construction of an organ and tells how to arrange the solo organ, echo organ, pedals, choir organ, etc. Part II has eleven chapters that describe in greater detail the manufacture of all the parts mentioned in Part I. Chapters 1-8, which provide advice for those who wish to have organs built, include information on the construction of the organ-case, manuals, bellows, pipes of various materials, etc. Chapter 9 summarizes the preceding chapters and deals with the mounting of the entire instrument. Chapter 10 takes up the voicing and tuning of the pipes and the problems encountered in making them speak together and sound harmonious. Advice about repairing and adding to organs and a description of a famous organ at the abbey of Weingarten in Germany are contained in chapter 11, which also has a section on organs without visible pipes. Part III presents much practical advice on what an organist (especially in the "provinces") needs to know about organ-builders and their work. Chapter 1 tells how to make up specifications for an organ builder and how to draw up a contract with one. A discussion of the inspection of organs and a model of the type of report an organist is expected to make appear in chapter 2. Chapter 3 takes up the maintenance of the organ, telling how to remedy some minor difficulties that are likely to arise. Chapter 4 gives about fifty registrations used by the most famous organists of Paris and states that any organist with taste can easily augment the number. Part IV describes in detail various types of organs and other instruments. Chapter 1 deals with organs suitable for rooms of different sizes, giving manual and pedal specifications for each. Chapter 2 is about table organs—simple, and with two ranks of pipes—while chapter 3 describes *Orgues à cylindre,* mechanical organs that can be played without a knowledge of music or performing technique. Chapter 4 tells how to make cylinders for use on the organs described in the third chapter, giving detailed directions, illustrated by charts, for specific pieces to be put on cylinders. In this chapter much information on performance practice is provided. Of especial interest are the comments on performance of notes written in equal values. These, Bédos de Celles says, are divided into two types of unequal value, *tenues* and *tactées.* The former are played "more or less prolonged"; of the latter "only the beginning of the note is expressed." Such notes normally succeed each other alternately in quarter-note values, in duple time, although the terms can also apply to eighth-notes and rarely to sixteenth-notes. In triple time the first note is *tenue*, the other two *tactées*. He treats this whole subject in much detail. There is also a brief section on ornamentation. Chapter 5 is about the pianoforte made at Paris by M. Lépine, organ-maker to the king, and chapters 6 and 7 discuss the ordinary *clavecin* and the viol briefly.

Facsimile ed. by Christhard Mahrenholz, in Series I of *Documenta musicologica* (1934-36). Foreword to Part IV in German (1793). Large parts of the work appear in German tr. in J. G. Töpfer, *Lehrbuch der Orgelbaukunst* (1855). See also C. Mahrenholz, *Die Orgelregister, ihre Geschichte und ihr Bau* (1930); Félix Raugel, *Recherches sur quelques maîtres de l'ancienne facture d'orgues française* (1925); C. Mahrenholz in *MGG*, I, 1494 ff.

72

JOHANN ERNST ALTENBURG. *Versuch einer Anleitung zur heroisch-musikalischen Trompeter- und Pauker-Kunst.* 1795.

The *Versuch* provides practically the only important testimony regarding the old art of the trumpet. At the end of a great tradition, Altenburg reveals the long-guarded secrets of the trumpeters' guild with learning, practical knowledge, good organization, and ready polemics. The work covers the historical foundation of the art, the guild organization, instruction, and performance practice.

An edition by R. Bertling (1911). See Arno Werner, "J. E. Altenburg, der letzte Vertreter der heroischen Trompeter- und Paukerkunst," *ZfMW*, XV (1933), 258.

73

HECTOR BERLIOZ. *Voyage musical en Allemagne et en Italie. Etudes sur Beethoven, Gluck, et Weber. Mélanges et nouvelles.* 1884.

This work is in part autobiography and in part music criticism. It consists of a series of essays on various musical subjects, these essays being grouped into five parts. Part I, "Voyage musical en Allemagne," describes the purpose and doctrine behind the revolutionary mission that Berlioz was undertaking in Germany at the time. Part II, "De la musique en général," is a formal definition of music. This was originally a contribution to an encyclopedia. Part III, "Etude analytique des symphonies de Beethoven," contains not only analyses of Beethoven's symphonies, but also a letter from Berlioz to Spontini, an account of the first performance of Weber's *Der Freischütz,* and other essays on the contemporary operatic scene. Part IV, "Voyage musical en Italie," is mainly an autobiographical account of Berlioz' musical adventures in Italy. It also contains three papers on Gluck's lyric dramas. Four critical essays on the tenor role in opera and on related operatic questions constitute Part V, "Astronomie musicale."

In a German tr. by J. C. Lobe (2 vols., n.d.). See Jacques Barzun, *Berlioz and the Romantic Century* (1950).

74

EDUARD HANSLICK. *Concerte, Componisten und Virtuosen der letzten fünfzehn Jahre.* 1886.

This volume contains a series of critical reviews by Hanslick of concerts given in Vienna between 1870 and 1885. The work, a chronologically arranged "concert-companion," is divided into fifteen parts, each reviewing the performances of a single year. The fifteen parts are in turn divided into sections, each being devoted to presentations of a specific type of music, such as orchestral music, chamber music, oratorios and other sacred music, etc. Among world *premières* reviewed are those of the first three symphonies of Brahms. Other works performed for the first time in Vienna and reviewed here are Brahms's *Variations on a Theme by Haydn* and the two piano concertos; Dvořák's *Slavonic Rhapsody for Orchestra, No. 3,* and *Trio in F minor for Piano and Strings;* Saint-Saëns' *Piano Concerto, Opus 22;* Tchaikovsky's *Romeo and Juliet Overture;* and the Prelude to Wagner's *Parsifal.* But the reviews are not confined to world *premières* or to first performances in Vienna. Many describe renditions of such works as Palestrina's *Stabat Mater,* Mendelssohn's *Reformation Symphony,* and Beethoven's *Eroica Symphony.* Among the virtuosos discussed are Franz Liszt, Clara Schumann, Hans von Bülow, Anton Rubinstein, Ferruccio Busoni, Joseph Joachim, Rafael Joseffy, and Xaver Scharwenka. Hanslick's resistance to the Liszt-Wagner movement is well known. On the other hand, he was an early supporter of Schumann and a strong adherent of Brahms. The reviews in the *Concerte, Componisten und Virtuosen* . . . vividly illustrate his dislikes and preferences.

See Eduard Hanslick, *Vienna's Golden Age of Music: 1850-1900,* tr. and ed. by Henry Pleasants (1951), which contains English trs. of a few reviews from the *Concerte, Componisten und Virtuosen* . . . ; Stewart Deas, *In Defence of Hanslick* (1940).

75

ALEXANDER S. FAMINTSIN. *Drevniaya Indo-Kitaiskaya Gamma v Asyi i Evrope . . . (The Ancient Indo-Chinese Scale in Asia and Europe, with Special Emphasis on its Manifestations in Russian Folk Songs).* 1889.

To quote Famintsin's own words, "the main object of this essay is to serve as a groundwork upon which one could erect more or less firmly a theoretical edifice of the Slavic folk melos." This, however, "is unthinkable without a comparative study of the structure, the fundamental laws, and the evolutionary history of the most essential scales that lie at the bottom of music practiced by various civilized nations. . . . We have confined ourselves in this essay to the ancient Indo-Chinese pentatonic, which has not only been used by some of the Old World nations since time immemorial, but to a considerable extent is employed by them in our own day." Following this brief preamble, Famintsin enters into a lengthy historical, ethnological, and musicological discussion concerning the use of the scale in question by the ancient Hindus, Chinese, Japanese, Mongolians, and some aboriginal tribes in Siberia and the vicinity of the Ural Mountains. This is complemented by further descriptions of similar scalar practices in ancient Greece and, later, in several northern countries such as Ireland, Scotland, and Brittany. This material occupies about two-thirds of the entire book, the remaining portion being dedicated to the scalar bases of Slavic folk songs as found in the various regions of Europe, but most of all in Russia. Despite this ultimate and apparently limited objective of the author, his long-range aim seems to have been also to prove that the pentatonic scale (sometimes with semitonal deflections) represents a universal prediatonic foundation in all the music of the world. The book itself is a pioneer scholarly contribution which, in its special field, remains to this day unparalleled—and in a large measure unchallenged—both within and outside of Russia. Although Famintsin's findings have been amplified by later discoveries and his occasionally obsolete views have been rectified, the musical and extra-musical discussions and the 137 music examples are important for all those interested in the general evolution of musical language, comparative studies of primitive musical cultures, formation of basic melodic formulas in folkloristic art, theoretical construction of scales, and the like, even though these specific branches of ethnomusicology are not always directly mentioned by the author.

76

HUGO WOLF. *Musikalische Kritiken*. 1911.

Wolf's critical reviews of the musical life of Vienna for more than three years were a feature of the fashionable weekly, the *Wiener Salonblatt*. The first, signed "x. y.," appeared on January 20, 1884. After that, articles under his own name appeared almost every Sunday during the concert and opera season until April 17, 1887. In these articles Wolf upholds Gluck, Mozart, Beethoven, and Wagner; defends Berlioz; scourges the modern Italians; breaks lances for Bruckner; and begins a bold campaign against Brahms. His real interest is in the operas of Gluck and Mozart, and the symphonies, chamber music, and sonatas of Beethoven. He writes, "Let Gluck, Mozart, and Wagner be for us the holy trinity that only in Beethoven becomes one." He loves Schubert, but finds flaws in him. The articles do not contain a great deal about Schumann, but Wolf's devotion is evident. He is always ready to discourse with authority upon all aspects of Wagnerian interpretation, problems of production and of performance, stage business, etc. He makes no comment upon the music of any of the Verdi operas that he heard as critic, but the weaker products of

Italian opera are torn to shreds. He undoubtedly overrates Liszt, but, apart from the undisguised antagonism to Brahms and those associated with the Brahmsian party, there is little in Wolf's critical writings that is unacceptable today.

Hugo Wolf's Musikalische Kritiken, ed. by Richard Batka and Heinrich Werner (1911). See Frank Walker, *Hugo Wolf* (1951); Kurt Varges, *Der Musikkritiker Hugo Wolf* (1934); and Romain Rolland, *Musicians of Today* (1915), pp. 168 ff.

77

VINCENT D'INDY. *Cours de composition musicale.* Book I, 1903; Book II: Part I, 1909; Part II, 1933.

Beginning with a discussion of Gregorian chant and extending through the symphonic poem, over 900 of the 1068 pages in these two books are devoted to an analysis of most of the important musical forms developed during the Christian era. The forms are discussed according to three large divisions in music history: the monophonic (rhythmic) period (3rd to 13th centuries); the polyphonic period (13th to 17th centuries); the metric period (17th to 20th centuries).

The *Cours* is divided into three parts. Book I covers the first two periods from the standpoints of notation, rhythm, melody, harmony, form, tonality, expression, and the application of the theory of harmony in the simultaneously performed melodies of the polyphonic era, and ends with a summary of what d'Indy regards as the progressive evolution of art, this summary leading up to brief comments on the metric period. In Book II, Part I, he defines symphonic and dramatic music and the forms inherent in each, includes a graphic table showing the development of these various forms either from Gregorian chant or from popular folk song arising from the dance, and studies the fugue, the suite, the sonata, and the variation as applied to keyboard instruments. Each chapter is divided into two sections, the technical and the historical.

The discussion of the forms examined in Book II, Part II, requires a preliminary knowledge of orchestral instruments. Therefore a brief treatment of the origin of orchestral instruments, their ranges, their capabilities, and the combinations possible, precedes an analysis of the concerto, symphony, chamber music, string quartet, symphonic overture, symphonic poem, and fantasy. Book III, in preparation by d'Indy's pupil, Auguste Sérieyx, who collaborated with d'Indy on the earlier volumes, will include a similar analysis of dramatic music, such as the opera, the oratorio, etc. The published volumes contain copious musical illustrations.

See Merle Montgomery, "A Comparative Analysis (and Translation) of Vincent d'Indy's *Cours de composition musicale,*" 7 vols., unpublished Ph.D. dissertation, University of Rochester (1946).

78

HEINRICH SCHENKER. *Neue musikalische Theorien und Phantasien.* 1906-1935. Volume I, *Harmonielehre* (1906); Volume II, *Kontrapunkt* (1910-1922); Volume III, *Der freie Satz* (1935; with a separate *Anhang* of examples).

In this work, his *magnum opus,* Schenker tries to reduce music to its most basic outline, which, according to him, consists of the *Ursatz* or fundamental harmonic framework, in the form of a two-part setting, the upper part of which is the *Urlinie,* a descending diatonic line. He divides music into a background (the melodic-harmonic essence), the middleground, and the foreground. The idea of key is enlarged so that modulations become excursions lying within the tonal orbit of one key. In brief, Schenker believes that all harmony must be related to the triad, that all melody must be related to the diatonic scale, and that all counterpoint can be reduced to a horizontal working-out of the triad.

Abridged English tr. of Vol. I, *Harmony*, by Oswald Jonas and Elizabeth M. Borgese (1954). See also M. Mann, "Schenker's Contribution to Music Theory," *The Music Review*, X (1949), 3. Schenker's theories are based entirely on music from Bach through Brahms. For attempts to widen their application, see F. Salzer, *Sinn und Wesen der abendländischen Mehrstimmigkeit* (1935) and *Structural Hearing* (1952).

79

ARNOLD SCHOENBERG. *Harmonielehre*. 1911 (enlarged 1922).

This comprehensive study of harmonic relations in the major-minor system was written after Schoenberg's thoroughgoing rejection of this system in his compositions. The fruit of his rich experience as a teacher (the opening sentence is: *Dieses Buch habe ich von meinen Schülern gelernt*), it is distinguished, above all, by the novelty of the pedagogical approach, rejecting both figured bass and melody harmonization as teaching methods in favor of the direct construction of harmonic progressions. The presentation is vivid and stimulating, mainly because of the numerous polemical and speculative side remarks which are valuable not only for their bearing on the subject but also for the insight they afford into the creative personality of one of the most influential musicians of our time. These portions, which are extraneous to a strictly formal presentation of the subject, are unfortunately omitted from Robert Adams' English translation (1948), as are the interesting conjectures concerning early atonal harmony with which the book concludes.

80

ALOIS HÁBA. *Neue Harmonielehre.* 1927.

This work, by one of the most important of the European progressivists, is divided into three exhaustive sections: I, melodic and harmonic basis of diatonic and chromatic tone systems—this material covering tonality, atonality, polytonality, tone-centers, and the whole-tone system; II, melodic and harmonic foundation of quarter-tone systems; III, melodic and harmonic foundation of third-tone, sixth-tone, and twelfth-tone systems. Each section is dealt with extensively and contains numerous examples.

The work is printed in the author's German translation from the original Czech.

AUTHOR INDEX

TITLE INDEX